D1500250

Religion and Human Experience
Number One

Harry M. Buck, *Series Editor*

ANIMA Books, 1982

The
Human
Way

A Dialogic
Approach to
Religion and
Human Experience

Via Humana

Maurice Friedman, Ph.D.

Library of Congress Cataloging in Publication Data

Friedman, Maurice
    The human way.

    Bibliography: p.
    1. Religion — Philosophy.   2. Philosophical anthropology.   I. Title.
BL51.F6818   200'.1   81-8011
ISBN 0-89012-025-0   AACR2

Printed in USA.

ANIMA BOOKS is a subdivision of Conococheague Associates, Inc., 1053
Wilson Avenue, Chambersburg, Pennsylvania 17201.

Foreword

THE FINAL DECADES of the twentieth century have been likened by some to an "Age of Isaac." Isaac's father, Abraham, "when he was called ... went out, not knowing where he was to go," perhaps thrilled to answer the call. His grandson, Jacob, fathered the first generation of the new People of the Lord, Israel. But Isaac stood between, at home neither in the old world or the new. Forbidden to marry a Canaanite woman but also unable to return home, a servant asked for Rebekah on his behalf. What courage she must have had to reply simply, "I will go."

In our day, as western civilization may be reaching its zenith, sensitive modern students of religion stand, like Isaac and Rebekah, between the ages. A growing awareness of the wholeness of human personality and intense interaction among previously discrete cultures have rendered obsolete many distinctions that served the past. It is increasingly unsatisfactory to view religion as a separate module of human experience because a need for meaningful commitment intrudes into virtually every modern reflection. Despite new vitality in religious institutions, the spiritual quest is no longer confined to church, synagogue, temple, or mosque. Nor can we understand it by focusing only on sacred literature.

The Human Way — Via Humana, as it was originally titled — inaugurates a new series of books on "Religion and Human Experience." Traditional approaches to our discipline developed early in this century, when biblical studies, theology, and the investigation of non-Christian religions were quite separate fields. George Foot Moore set the pattern in 1913 when his *History of Religions* divided the spiritualities of the world into various "religions." Each decade thereafter has seen "new" textbooks describing religions of the world.

Professor Friedman's book is refreshingly different, a fresh assessment of lived Reality. Like Rebekah, he has answered, "I will go" where the path may lead. Like Isaac, he mediates between tradition and modernity. Whatever else may be involved, here we see religion as human experience which involves total persons in total responses to what is viewed as ultimate Reality, to quote Joachim Wach, Friedman's teacher and mine. There is a growing network of discerning men and women from diverse backgrounds seeking dialogue as they discover "touchstones" to enrich their spiritual journey. As its subtitle indicates, this volume, as well as the series it initiates, provides "a dialogic approach to religion and human experience." It never calls for discarding our separate and separating heritages, but it summons us to stand *on* them instead of being buried beneath them.

Journey through the world of experience involves many relationships: to transcendent Reality, to the earth itself, and in particular in dialogue with other persons. Dr. Friedman addresses these relationships, seeing religion neither as an objective philosophy nor as a subjective experience only, but as a lived reality, "a basic attitude or relationship arising in the encounter with the whole reality directly given to one in one's existence" (page 4).

Harry M. Buck
Series Editor

Preface

The Human Way: A Dialogical Approach to Religion and Human Experience has come into existence thanks to the promptings of Harry M. Buck, professor of religion studies at Wilson College, editor of the journal ANIMA, director of Anima Press, and former executive director of the American Academy of Religion.

In October 1974 Harry Buck wrote to me of the impact of my book Touchstones of Reality, which he had just read in its paperback edition (Dutton Books): "I scarcely remember any book that spoke more directly to my own spiritual condition." In the same letter, he brought to my attention a series of books on Religion and Human Experience that he was planning to edit and later, when I responded positively to his interest, wrote that he would like me to write a book that would head the series.

At a recent conference entitled "Philosophy, Where Are You?" an old friend took me to task for publicly acknowledging my indebtedness to him for introducing me, 35 years ago, to Berdyaev, Bergson, Kierkegaard, Heidegger, and, above all, Martin Buber, whose book I and Thou combined mysticism and social action and would, he hoped, check my tendency to move away from socialism and social action to immersion in mysticism. "Philosophy," he instructed me, "has nothing to do with the personal." To me, philosophy has everything to do with the personal. I do not say, as Hans Jonas does, that Martin Heidegger is a gnostic, though Jonas' claim for this statement is impressive. But when I am told that Heidegger's active political Nazism from 1933 to 1936 and the integral relation of his philosophy of the 1930s to his Nazi speeches of that time (as I have demonstrated at length in Part VII of *The Worlds of Existentialism*) are irrelevant to his philosophy, then I feel that I am, indeed, confronted by a dualism between the higher reaches of gnosis and the world in which we live. Martin Buber's statement that "[dualistic] religion is the great enemy of mankind" might equally well be applied to this approach to philosophy!

My approach to philosophy is necessarily personal. This does not mean that it is subjective, emotional, or distorted. It means, rather, that I am committed to it and invested in it, that what I put forward is not only scholarship but also personal insight and personal conviction. It means that although I do not speak from the standpoint of any one religious tradition, the illustrations that I give in this book are from the religions that I have personally entered into dialogue with.

The reader of *The Human Way* will find more references to Hasidism, the popular communal Jewish mysticism of eighteenth and nineteenth century East European Jewry, than to any other religious tradition, with Taoism and Zen Buddhism coming in a close second. This does not mean that I speak as a representative of Judaism or Hasidism, for I am neither a rabbi nor a Hasid; I do not even belong to a synagogue or temple. What I represent is a *dialogical approach to religion and human experience*, and this approach cannot be confined to any one religion. Nonetheless, because I have carried on an active dialogue with the tales of the Hasidim for a great many years, more illustrations have come to my mind from there than anywhere else.

I do not claim to have done justice to any one religion and still less to all. I speak not only as a historian and philosopher of religion, but also as the person I am, with the *touchstones of reality* that have become mine over the years. It is my hope that the readers of this book will be able to enter into a dialogue with my touchstones in such a way that they can apply to their own touchstones and their own traditions and fields of scholarship the insights and issues that I present.

Because of the special task of this book — making explicit the new philosophy of religion implicit in *Touchstones of Reality* — on a number of occasions I have found it necessary to repeat insights, concepts, and even passages from this earlier book. In a few cases this has been true also of *Martin Buber: The Life of Dialogue, To Deny Our Nothingness: Contemporary Images of Man* and of *The Hidden Human Image.* But in every case I have done so in a different context, for a different purpose, and therefore with an altered and enriched meaning.

I wish to thank my friend and student Cherlyn Davis for her suggestion that I include a chapter on religious leadership. I am deeply indebted to Harry Buck for his many invaluable editorial suggestions.

Solana Beach, California
August , 1980

Maurice Friedman

Table of Contents

Part one

Introduction:
The Heartland of Religion

1

Approaching Religious Reality through Touchstones

Inasmuch as truth and falsehood have been mingled, and the good and bad coin have been poured into the travelling-bag. Therefore they need a picked touchstone, one that has undergone [many] tests in [assaying] realities.

Jalálu'ddin Rúmi, thirteenth century Sufi mystic

I F THE DEFINITION of philosophy is itself a philosophical problem, as Paul Tillich says, then the definition of philosophy of religion is still more so. It depends on one's understanding of the task of philosophy, one's brand of epistemology, one's definition of religion, and one's intuition of ontology.

Philosophy for me, as for Heraclitus, Socrates, Plato, and Aristotle, is the love of wisdom, the examination of life in search of authentic existence, and the investigation of the interrelation of being, knowing, and valuing. The epistemology that makes most sense to me arises from the meeting of self and other, the impact of otherness within a relation of direct mutual contact, the dialectical alternation of the immediacy of direct mutual knowing and the indirect knowledge that objectifies and categorizes yet need not prevent the return to dialogical knowing. Ontology for me is best grasped as an intuition of the *between* — the relational — that can be pointed to but cannot be understood entirely from outside the meeting in which the between becomes manifest. Religion, for me, is neither an objective philosophy nor a subjective experience. It is a lived reality that is ontologically prior to its expression in creed, ritual, and group. At the same time it is inseparable from these expressions and cannot be distilled out and objectified. The *religious* at this deepest level might be described as a basic *attitude* or relationship arising in the encounter with the whole reality directly given to one in one's existence. The task of philosophy of religion for me is a conceptual clarification and a metaphorical pointing to the religious reality that is known in the between but without abstracting from that meeting detached statements about the nature and attributes of God and without doing injustice to the typical and the unique apprehended in the phenomenological study of the history of religions.

My own philosophy of religion, which I shall attempt to make explicit in the subsequent chapters of this book, *The Human Way*, is already implicit in my earlier book *Touchstones of Reality*: first, an autobiographical section where I tell of my responses to the historical events of my time in the progressive stages through which I moved — not without great anguish — from liberalism to socialism to pacifism to mysticism and finally, without discarding any of the others, to what I called, long before Erikson used the term, "basic trust"; second, a large section on my dialogue with some of the great religions — Hinduism, early Buddhism, Zen, Taoism, Biblical faith, Hasidism, the Jesus of the Gospels, and Quakerism; third, a section in which I give my responses to the crisis of values, to the claim of psychology to interpret religion, to the new social ethic that I see emerging from my dialogue with the religions, and to the "covenant of peace"; and, fourth, the partnership of existence, the courage to address and to respond, and a meaning for modern man.
In this chapter, I wish to indicate briefly some of the various insights of philosophers, mystics, and novelists that I have made my own and follow them with a brief overview of touchstones of reality as an approach to the philosophy of religion.

I do not follow Plato's harmony of the chord but *Heraclitus'* harmony of opposing tension — the bow and the lyre. "That which is alone One is willing and not willing to be called Zeus." "The oracle at Delphi neither speaks nor conceals but indicates." "The eyes and ears are bad witnesses for men with barbarian souls." *Meister Eckhart* prays for the uniqueness of each one of us; sees God as the great self-sharer; declares that when God laughs at the soul and the soul laughs back at God, the Trinity is born; and witnesses: "God is nearer to me than I am to myself. My being depends on God's intimate presence." *Blaise Pascal* sees man as a finite middle between the infinite and the infinitesimal, as a limited being who is neither all nor nothing. He contrasts knowing about God with loving God: "The heart has reasons that reason knows not." *Friedrich Nietzsche* proclaims the Self as a mighty lord, an unknown sage behind our thoughts and feelings. He sees man as the valuing animal and declares that without valuation the nut of existence is hollow. He unmasks the "will to truth" as the will to thinkableness of all being, the will to make existence smooth and rational; for we doubt with good reason that it is so. Nietzsche too understands the unique. "This — is now *my* way — where is yours?" Zarathustra answers those who ask him about *the* way. "As for *the* way, it does not exist."

Franz Rosenzweig, the twentieth-century German-Jewish existentialist, celebrates the "New Thinking" that sprang up in many different thinkers at the end of the First World War. The "New Thinking" is dialogue, not monologue. It recognizes that the other has not only ears but also a mouth, that the other can say something that can surprise you, and that thinking and knowing as a result are bound to time. That which is truth is true for some one. It is verified and realized in actual life, from mathematical truths that are verified with the mind alone, to existential truths that have to be paid for even at the cost of life or of generations. Much more important for me than the influence of Rosenzweig, however, was that of two other Jewish existentialists — *Abraham Joshua Heschel*, with his philosophy of wonder, and *Martin Buber*, with his philosophy of dialogue. To explore life leads to the unfathomable, to deny it to nothingness. "If you hallow this life, you meet the living God." Real faith is not a *what* but a question and answer, address and response that cannot be divorced from the unique situation. Faith is a "happening but once" that is lived and tested in the stream alone. Meaning, to Buber, is open and accessible in the "lived concrete" — not through existential analysis or aiming at experiencing, which destroys spontaneity, but through standing firm before the whole might of reality and answering it in a living way.

Writing my book, *Problematic Rebel*, which is based on an intensive dialogue with Melville, Dostoevsky, and Kafka, was a steppingstone to my philosophy of religion. "The only really difficult and insoluble problems," writes *Franz Kafka*, "are those which we cannot formulate, because they have the difficulties of life itself as their content." To me Kafka is the existentialist of the call and of the calling to account that comes when we do not answer the call. "It is entirely conceivable that life's splendor forever lies in wait about each one of us in all its fulness, but veiled from view, deep down, invisible, far off. It is there, though, not hostile, not reluctant, not deaf. If you summon it by the right word, by its right name, it will come." Kafka abjures the path of the metaphysicians and theologians who speak of God or the Absolute as if knowledge of ultimate reality were possible apart from our relation to it. But he also abjures the negative metaphysics of Nietzsche and Sartre who proclaim that "God is dead." Instead, he encourages us to stand face to face with the reality that one must confront yet can see only from the ground on which the concrete, existing person stands.

In *Problematic Rebel*, I have distinguished two types of modern rebel — the *Modern Promethean* and the *Modern Job*. These two do not correspond to unbelief and belief but rather to a programmatic mistrust that demands the All or the Nothing (a total recovery of man's alienated freedom from whatever other confronts him) and a mixture of trust and contending, which faithfully confronts the given even while opposing and contending with it. The question of existential trust at the heart of the contending of the biblical Job is also at the heart of the *Problematic Rebel*. But Captain Ahab and Ivan Karamazov have "turned their tickets in," while Kafka's K. (*The Castle*) and Camus' Dr. Rieux (*The Plague*) still affirm the meaning that emerges in the Dialogue with the Absurd. The rebellion of the Modern Job, like that of the Modern Prometheus, may be the atheism of Camus or the theism of Buber: in both, dialogue and rebellion are coupled. "My God will not allow to be silent in the mouth of his creature the protest against the great injustice of the world," writes Buber, and Camus proclaims the rebellion that remains within the dialogue between person and person. Today, as we learn both from the world of modern physics and from Auschwitz and Hiroshima, meaning can be found only through the attitude of the person who is willing to *live* with the absurd, remaining open to the mystery that we cannot pin down.

The concept of touchstones of reality implies no prior definition of reality nor any metaphysical absolute. Yet touchstones of reality cannot be reduced to any current form of subjectivism — whether it be that of cultural relativism, psychologism, Freudian psychoanalysis, behaviorism, Sartrian existentialism, or linguistic analysis. There is no *touch* independent of contact with *otherness*, an otherness that transcends subjectivity even though it cannot be known without it. The coloration of the *Zeitgeist* that seals us within our cultural subjectivity is not a touchstone of reality but fool's gold. Touchstones of reality must be made true ever again by testing them in each new situation — bringing the life-stance they have produced into a moment of present reality. Unlike scientific generalizations, touchstones of reality provide valid insights confirmable in some situations but not all. Touchstones of reality are closer to events than insights. They provide no secure purchase above the stream of living. We are left with the problem of when to move in the direction of insight and abstraction and when to move back into the living waters.

The approach of touchstones of reality is nowhere more fruitful than in trying to understand religion. The great error is to see religion as proof of the existence of God or as a description of God's nature or attributes. Religion is the way that one walks. It is a commitment, a life-stance. It is one's basic response to life whether or not one affirms the existence of God. Our dialogue with religions is not a search for *the* truth, accordingly — either Plato's absolute or the one true religion or the "perennial philosophy." Each religion speaks of its uniqueness, and each says something to us about our life as humankind and as the unique persons we are. The answer to the dilemma of religious particularism versus religious universalism, consequently, is the *mutually confirming pluralism of touchstones of reality*. In contrast to the overclaim of absolute truth and the underclaim of subjective relativism, touchstones of reality witness to as much reality as we can witness to at any given moment.

Both touchstones of reality and the dialogue of touchstones imply the *partnership of existence* (the title of a chapter in *Touchstones of Reality*). The partnership of existence was already fully explicit in the Taoism of Lao-tzu, and it is also strongly emphasized in Hasidism. We cannot find our touchstones by remaining with ourselves or by making ourselves the goal. We know ourselves only in responding to others. This response to otherness means becoming whole in responding, and this means in turn giving direction to our passion in meaningful relationship, or, as the Hasidim say, serving God with the "evil" urge. This does not imply taking part in evil or even integrating good and evil through one's individuation, but making decision with one's whole being.

The ultimate product of our movement from touchstone to touchstone and our dialogue of touchstones in the partnership of existence is the *community of otherness*. I distinguish two types of community — one of affinity and one of otherness. The community of affinity, or likemindedness, is based on what people feel they have in common — race, sex, religion, nationality, politics, a common class, a common creed. The community of otherness, in contrast, is based on common situation, common caring, and common concern. It does not mean that everyone does the same thing and certainly not that they do it from the same point of view. What makes such a community real is people who understand that their shared concerns call each of them to respond by different but still genuine paths. The very existence in genuine community is already a common concern, a caring for one another. This caring begins with understanding from within the actual people present. Only then does it extend to gathering other people in and then to a dialogue with other communities.

Community of affinity, or likemindedness, is always ultimately false community because its members do not relate to one another directly and they do not confirm one another in their personal uniqueness but only in their function of bolstering one another's security. Community of otherness is a way of being faithful and diverse at the same time. The alternative to absolutist trust and hopeless relativism is the trust that affirms religious pluralism as the starting point of any serious modern faith. We must give up looking for the "one true religion" and see that religious commitments, even of people in the same church or synagogue, are unique relationships to a truth which we cannot possess.

The partnership of existence and the community of otherness imply in their turn *existential trust*. I can go forth ever again to meet present reality, but I cannot control the form in which I shall meet it. *Idolatry* is the attempt to limit the partnership of existence to a given form, condition, or image. Existential trust, in contrast, enables us to go out to new meeting and again become whole, alive, present. Existential trust gives actuality and continuity to our discontinuous relationships and enables the individual course of existence to become a personal direction rather than a meaningless flux. It accepts the fact that genuine relationship is two-sided and beyond the control of our will, hence that there are no guarantees written in the heart of the universe. To make existential trust real in our lives we need the courage to address and the courage to respond — to meet the reality given in this moment, whatever its form, because here only is meaning accessible to us, even if not without horror, suffering, and evil. The courage to address and respond is sapped by *existential mistrust*, which grows out of the loss of trust in the meeting with the other. Trust in God is ultimately identical with existential trust, for the latter is not trust that existence is constituted one way rather than another but the willingness to confront reality moment by moment as it comes.

It is possible to hold in tension touchstones of reality that seem to contradict each other, but there are also choices of priorities that must be made along the road. Touchstones of reality are not universal ideals shining above history; rather they are existential realities that are meaningful only as shared, witnessed for, and made living again in the present. We receive from each other without ever being identical, and we grow through this receiving, each in our own way. Realizing this may help us distinguish between two different kinds of meaning: a comprehensive world view and the meaning inherent in an event of meeting. A world view is not necessary for living as a human being, and it may get in the way of our confrontation with the concrete and rob us of the real world. We meet the "eternal Thou" only in our existence as persons, only in our meeting with the other. We cannot know it from outside existence.

What then is the relationship of touchstones of reality to "truth"? There is no absolute truth other than our relationship to each present moment. Yet into that relationship may enter every other truth relationship that we have made our own. Our truth relationships do not yield a higher truth that can be objectivized as always the same, but they do yield touchstones that stand the test of new situations, and from these touchstones arise religious insights and philosophical formulations.

2

The Insight of the Religions
into the Problem of Human Existence

Wonders are many, but none are so wondrous as man.

Sophocles, Antigone

You could not in your going find the ends of the soul, though you travelled the whole way: so deep is its *Logos*.

Heraclitus of Ephesus

What is man that Thou art mindful of him?
  And the son of man that Thou dost care for him?

Psalm 8

MY MOST IMPORTANT source for touchstones as an approach to religious reality has been my dialogue with some of the world's great religions, particularly through their scriptures. (In sharing this dialogue I am making no attempt to be comprehensive or even to give an adequate presentation of the religions that I do treat; nor do I in any way intend to disparage those religions that I do not include.)

What is common to all great religions is that each in its own way sees human existence as a problem to itself. Why?

Because of the givens of human existence — the awareness of self, the passage of time, change, the inexorable and irreversible movement from youth to age to death; possibility and the need for choice; freedom and the checks on freedom by the limitation of our inner resources and the constraint of our natural and social environment; one's dual existence in self-relationship and interpersonal relationship, in inner awareness and outer social role; one's dual consciousness in waking and sleeping, in languor and intensity — all these in themselves make human existence problematic. Through all of them there run discontinuities and confusions that force the human being to seek a reality amidst appearance, a stability amidst flux, an order amidst chaos, a meaning amidst paradox and incongruity. What is the self? What is time? What is reality? What is life and death? What is consciousness and what is the essence of the objective world? These questions have been an integral part of all human existence from the earliest times till today.

Hinduism's special contribution to our understanding of the problem of the fully human, is its profound insights into consciousness and subjectivity, and the relation of these to inner energy, motivation, and concentration and to the nature, meaning, and effectiveness of human action. All these factors come together into what we might call a progress toward absolute subjectivity — the essential reality of the Self and its identity with ultimate reality.

We can understand this progress to absolute subjectivity in terms of our common experiences in which the dreamer is more real than the dream; in which the continuity of the self is set in contrast to the flux of the world that the self witnesses; in which we are aware of the consciousness as detached from the senses, when we concentrate so much on a certain matter that, although our auditory senses are fully functioning, we do not hear the world around us. Though music is playing, we do not hear the music. Though someone may call our names, we do not hear it. This is true with all the other senses too. We can look and yet not see anything because we are intent on something else. If we can thus withdraw the consciousness from the senses, we can conceive of the mind remaining within itself without going out to the senses. If we follow this through, we discover that consciousness is not, as we often think, simply a matter of sensation — that, apart from sensation, consciousness exists itself as something pure, something *sui generis*, something in itself. So the mystic experiences consciousness in the state that seems beyond time, beyond place, beyond awareness of itself — a state of pure consciousness, resting and dwelling in consciousness. Yet the mystic knows that in some way this very consciousness also enters into the perception of the world to which he or she relates. Thus the very beginning point of the Hindu yoga of meditation is the withdrawal of consciousness from the senses into the mind, leading to inner illumination.

In the Upanishads, the progress to an absolute essence of the self and the idealist emphasis on the witness as more real than what is witnessed is coupled with an analysis that reduces objective reality from particular objects to the categories in which those objects are seen and then from these categories to undifferentiated essence, so that *nama-rupa* — the world of name and form — disappears into the Absolute. The world of particulars is seen to be nothing but waves on the ocean of reality. Through this method the objective world is reduced to one essence and reality, just as the self is reduced to one essence and reality. Only when we progressively back away from the categories and from the world of particulars are we ready to arrive at that awareness of identity that is at the root of the mystical experience. The philosophy itself does not give one the experience, but it may be a necessary preparation for it — for the final leap — just as in Plato's *Republic* the dialectic of the philosopher leads him out of the cave up the hill to the top of the hill where he then makes the leap to the sun, which represents the direct knowledge of the Good, the True, and the Beautiful.

Having arrived at these two separate points, the absolute subjective essence within the self and the absolute objective essence of reality, then through a combination of direct mystical experience and philosophical contemplation stimulated by that experience, the two aspects of absolute subjectivity (*Atman*, or the Self) and absolute objectivity (*Brahman*) are identified. In a lightning flash there arises the central insight of the Upanishads and of the whole nondualistic Vedanta: *Brahman* is *Atman, tat twam asi* — Thou art That. *Brahman* is the impersonal Absolute, the One without Second. It must in no way be identified either with God as we know Him in the Western tradition or with any particular Hindu deity. Quite beyond our concepts, it can only be known as "not-two," or sometimes as *Sat Chit Ananda Brahman* — Being, Consciousness, Bliss Absolute.

The statement that Brahman is Atman is the statement that this objective universal reality out there is identical with the Self discovered within. From this basic insight, the whole system of Vedanta philosophy developed. This whole religious approach begins with the intense need, the wholly concentrated desire to find one's true way. "The good is one thing, the pleasant another," Death tells Nachiketas in the Katha Upanishad. Those who seek after pleasure will always be deluded. To say this is to say that there is a life of appearances and a life of reality. It is to say, as Socrates says to the Athenians, "Are you not ashamed that you value the things that are *not* valuable, like money, fame, and prestige, and you do not value the things that are truly valuable? You do not value your soul." Or in the words of Jesus, "What doth it profit a man to gain the whole world if he lose his soul?" "Only when man shall roll up the sky like a hide," says a Upanishad, "will there be an end of misery, unless this truth has first been known." No greater contrast could be found to the epicurean view, which looks on pleasure as the sole meaning and the only possible fulfillment of life. The *Gayatri mantram*, perhaps the most famous Hindu prayer, begins, "From the unreal lead us to the real, from darkness to light, from death to immortality."

The aim of Hinduism is not just enlightenment, *samadhi*, but *moksha*, liberation, freedom from rebirth. This liberation comes only when one gets rid of all the *karma* from one's past lives and fulfills one's *dharma*. *Dharma* is the cosmic order; it is the law that governs it; it is also your individual destiny through all your lives within the order. *Karma* is what you build up from your actions in each life; for these determine what befalls you and what you must rise above in your next life. It is not enough to be a good, or moral, person. You have to work through even that.

But you cannot leap "beyond good and evil." You have to follow the order to get beyond it. Hinduism at its fullest is thus at one and the same time both a cosmic religion and an acosmic one.

The most central Hindu scripture is the *Bhagavad-Gita*, the "Song of the Lord." The *Gita* is a philosophy of action based on the insight of the Upanishads and on the experience of countless seekers. Perhaps the central statement in the *Gita* is "He who sees the action that is in inaction, the inaction that is in action is wise indeed." The "action that is in inaction" is the effectiveness of the person who does not seem to act, who does not interfere in the world arbitrarily, and yet acts out of the wholeness, the fullness, the concentration of his being, out of the spiritual state that he has reached. The inaction that is in action is the ineffectiveness of the busy, active person — the typical Western political, social worker, or anyone, for that matter, who rushes around thinking that if he does more and more things, he is accomplishing more and more. What is at stake here is not merely the accomplishment of a goal, but the total meaning. One cannot realistically speak of the goal and the way to the goal as separate entities. The Hindus speak of *apūrva*, a subtle cause. One's actions begin as gross and become subtle so that one is not aware of them. Yet they have their effect, whether for good or for evil. So to the Hindu the old argument about means and ends is radically transformed. Everything has its effect: if one uses a good means, it will have a good effect; if one uses a bad means, it will have a bad effect. The aim is not merely the piling up of external structures, but inner spiritual growth and enlightenment.

Buddhism's special contribution to our understanding of the problem of the fully human is its insight into suffering and its emphasis on mindfulness, wisdom, and compassion. The Buddha was a greater social revolutionary than Gandhi, for he rejected the Hindu caste system. For the Buddha, a Brahmin was not a man who has a certain caste-mark on his forehead, but any man who is noble in character and action. The *Arhat*, or disciple, follows the noble way. He begins with the four noble truths: all existence is suffering; suffering is caused by old age, birth, and death; these are caused in turn by our craving for existence; and the way to liberation from suffering is the Eightfold

Path. The Buddha preserved from Hinduism the ideas of karma and reincarnation, but he did not hold existence to be illusion. On the contrary, it is all too real. We must find the way that will liberate us from this suffering by liberating us from our craving for existence. This way is the Eightfold Path: right views, right resolution, right speech, right action, right livelihood, right will, right mindfulness, and right meditation. Right mindfulness is not moral judgment but the simple awareness of what one is doing and feeling at every moment that gives us detachment from it: "Now I am walking. Now I am standing. Now I am feeling lust."

Whereas Hinduism, if only with negatives, points to an Absolute, to Brahman, the One without Second, and says, "This is a reality compared to which this world is an illusion," one does not find in early Buddhism any positing of an absolute. Nirvana, so far as the Buddha describes it, is simply backing away from the world in progressive stages until you no longer are there in it. The tendency to identify religion with finding the answers to "ultimate questions" — Is there immortality? Does God exist? — is thrown aside in early Buddhism in favor of a purely pragmatic view of action. The Buddha's concern is what counts now, what matters now, and the rest are "questions that tend not to edification." Why bother with these things? This teaching stands in contrast with the Western, the Hindu, and even the later Buddhist fondness for metaphysics.

The emphasis in early Buddhism, therefore, is not upon knowledge. It is not upon discovering what is the nature of the cosmos or the acosmos that includes or is identical with man. The emphasis is anthropological, it is human. It makes no statement about reality, except one thing; that it changes. "All things change, all things perish, all things pass away." If we try to hold on to any part of existence, we will suffer. Our very enjoyment of this moment must mean our suffering and sadness in the next moment. It cannot but be so. If we were able to enjoy the moment, relate to it, and then let it go, that would be different. But something else happens. Not only do we have this momentary relation, but then we fix it: we record the fact that this was a pleasurable sensation or that this was painful. Thus, at a later time, we are drawn to this sensation or we shrink from it. As a result we are not able to accept the simplest and most elementary fact of human existence — that all things change, perish, and pass away. Human life is a vain search for building security. We try fruitlessly to shore it up in every direction, like Kafka's mole who is never done fortifying his hole.

The Buddhist may be characterized as a "stream uprunner" — one who applies his will, who is going to end his craving for existence, who is going to attain enlightenment, who is going to overcome death and rebirth. Where have we ever seen a religion that laid out its way with such logical clarity: existence is suffering, suffering is caused by craving, the way to overcome craving is the eightfold path? The "compassionate Buddha" always remained close to the concrete situation, to the pragmatic problem at hand, "How can we help ourselves escape from suffering?" This closeness to the concrete is renewed in sophisticated and paradoxical form in Zen — the form of Mahayana Buddhism that grew out of the most abstruse philosophies of "mind only," "the void," "suchness," and the interpenetration of all reality.

Religion is often taken to be a movement away from mundane reality to the spirit floating above it. Zen Buddhism says no such movement is possible: there is only the one reality of spirit and sense. It says, secondly, that it is our reason that has created the impression that there are these separate worlds of spirit and sense-intellect. This differs strikingly from Hinduism with its statement that this world is *maya*, or illusion, and that Brahman is reality. Instead, we have the remarkable statement that the "one" and the "ten thousand things" are identical, that "nirvana *is* samsara [birth and death]." It is our minds that bifurcate existence into body and spirit, the one and the many. We cannot overcome our existential dilemma by fleeing from the many to the one; for this very attempt to overcome dualism leads us to still another dualism — that of the one as opposed to the many. One must instead go right to the concrete particular that at the same time is the Buddha Nature. There is no process here of abstracting from concrete reality, of uncovering the essence and shucking off this world. There is no world of name and form that is to be understood as merely that and therefore illusion. On the contrary, the very particularity of things, their very name and form, is the only means through which one can attain enlightenment. One finds the "essence" just as much in the movement of the world as in the nonmovement. In that sense, Zen is like Taoism: it does not cling to one opposite or the other.

It is impossible for us to meditate on any reality, religious or otherwise, without pointing to it. Through these pointers — words, symbols, myths, even rituals, we enable ourselves to return again and again to the insight or the contact we have achieved. But then the second step always follows: the tendency to regard the pointer as the reality and to lose what it is pointing toward. The Vedantists and the early Mahayana Buddhists were on the right track in trying to overcome the idea that things are divided up into myriads of discriminate things, but they did not go far enough. By saying "Reality is the 'not-two'" they fell into a world of intellectual discrimination between the one and the ten-thousand things. As a Zen text puts it, "They take the finger pointing to the moon for the moon itself."

There is much in both Zen Buddhism and Taoism that raises serious questions about the assumption of most of the intellectual currents of the nineteenth and twentieth centuries that *analysis* is the way to reach reality. If I take a thing apart into its supposed parts, have I thereby grasped this thing? Only if I assume that all things are really reducible to their component parts. Which often means, only if I have already found what I believe to be the basic reality — such as a Marxist dialectic or a form of economic determinism or Freud's or Jung's theory of the libido or the analytic categories of the linguistic philosopher. The way is right there before you, but you are going to miss it if you say that perceptions are all illusion or if you take perceptions as the material for your analysis. Much of what is called "existential" philosophy in our day — Heidegger, Sartre, even Tillich — starts with existence but then goes on to analyze it into phenomenological categories. Unlike Zen Buddhism, it does not stay with the concrete, but quickly leaves it to go to one realm or another and thereby perhaps loses the really existential quality that does not yield itself to analysis.

To get the flavor of Zen, you have to grasp its paradoxical, concrete quality — the tension of the border between inner and

outer that avoids simple immersion in things and quietistic sub-
mergence in the within. There is no denial of the senses in Zen.
When enlightenment has come, nothing is changed except one's
relation to it. If we are talking about ultimates, we are talking
about what transcends, includes, or undergirds all systems and is
not included within them. There is no basic philosophy of religion that is not paradoxical, therefore, including the nondualist
philosophy of the Vedanta, founded as it is on the paradox that
we not only take *maya* to be reality but that it is indeed as real
as creation, for creation itself is a paradoxical union of the utter
Absolute with the world of the relative. But the Zen Buddhists
retain their paradoxicality right down to the particular. It is a
part of their life-style, their touchstone of reality.

Less intense and less paradoxical than Zen, but no less a mysticism of the concrete and the particular, is Taoism. The center of
Taoism is the Tao — the way of life and the way of man in
which one finds the "natural" course that flows with the stream
rather than runs against it. Taoism accepts the opposites of *Yin*
and *Yang* — feminine and masculine, dark and light, earth and
heaven, receptive and active — without insisting upon one or the
other. It does not hold them in tension but swings easily from
one to the other. Hence its action is *wu-wei*, the action of the
whole being that has the appearance of non-action because it
does not intervene or interfere. This action seems most effortless
just when it is most effective.

The sane person is the one who does not try to capture existence as a whole within the limited, and of limited usefulness,
categories of analysis, whether scientific, psychoanalytic, or linguistic. Life reveals itself in its images if one opens oneself to the
image in such depth that one allows it to speak — as every image
does — of its source.

The Hindu notion of creation as *lila*, or "the play of the gods,"
has been rightly interpreted by Alan Watts and others as "sitting
lightly to the world," though this attitude only truly comes to
those who have gone through and beyond the order and attained
enlightenment. The history religions, Judaism, Christianity, and
Islam, speak not of divine sport but of divine destiny — in the
sense that God himself has a stake in creation, in history. History

here is not the cyclical history that we see in the notion of the *kalpas* and *yugas* of Hinduism and the Great Year of ancient Greek religion. Rather it is linear, a line that stretches from creation to redemption, even though neither the beginning nor the end can be understood as a moment in time. Instead of an event being merely a part of a cycle or spiral, every event has its own uniqueness and its own meaning. "Meaning is open and accessible in the lived concrete." We do not have to put away the world of the senses, or nature, or time, or history to find this meaning.

At the center of the faith of *biblical Judaism* stands not belief, in the ordinary sense of the term, but *emunah*, trust — a trust that no exile from the presence of God is permanent, that each person and each generation is able to come into contact with reality. In the life of the individual person, as of generations, it is the movement of time — the facts of change and death — that most threatens this trust. Every great religion, culture, and philosophy has observed that "all is flux" and that man himself is a part of this flux. The conclusions that have been drawn from this fact, however, are as different as the world views of those who have drawn the conclusions. The response of biblical man has not taken the form of a cyclical order of time or an unchanging absolute, like the Greek, nor of the dismissal of time and change as *maya*, or illusion, like the Hindu, or of the notion that one may flow with time, like the Taoist. Biblical man stands face to face with the changing creation and receives each new moment as an address of God — the revelation that comes through the unique present.

To stand before eternity is to be aware of one's own mortality:

> For a thousand years in thy sight are but as yesterday when it is past, ... men ... are like a dream, like grass ... in the morning it flourishes and is renewed; in the evening it fades and withers....
> Our years come to an end like a sigh ... yet their span is but toil and trouble; they are soon gone, and we fly away.
> (Psalm 90:4-10)

This is the universal human condition — a condition that has tempted some to see existence as unreal or as an ephemeral reflection of reality and others to "eat, drink, and be merry, for to-morrow we die." The psalmist, in contrast, prays that he may withstand this reality and heighten it, that he may make his existence real by meeting each new moment with the wholeness of his being:

> So teach us to number our days
> That we may get a heart of wisdom. (Psalm 90:12)

It is not only mortality, but also the suffering of the innocent and the prosperity of the wicked that leads to the tempering of trust in Job and in the Psalms. The reaffirmation of trust takes place out of an immediate sense of exile. Job and the Psalmist cannot bear the fact that the presence of God is emptied out of the world, that the sinners who cannot stand in the judgment are nonetheless confirmed by the congregation, and thus divine and social reality are split asunder. It is out of this situation that Job cries out and contends with a strength perhaps unequalled in any of the world's religious scriptures.

The basic paradox of the Hebrew Bible is the dialogue between eternal God and mortal human, between the imageless Absolute and we who are created in God's image. If that dialogue is to take place, it must take place not in eternity but in the present — in the unique situation of a limited human being who was born yesterday and will die tomorrow. Jacob wrestles with the angel, and Job wrestles with God, to receive the blessing of this dialogue on which the very meaning of their existence depends. Job holds fast to his trust in the real God whom he meets in the dreadful fate that has befallen him, and he holds fast to the facts of his innocence and his suffering. At the heart of the Book of Job stands neither blind faith nor denial of God, but trusting and contending: Job recognizes his dependence on God yet stands firm on the ground of his created freedom.

The balance of Job's "He may slay me, I await it,/But I will argue my ways before him" is repeated in the Hasidic Rabbi Bunam's saying, "Every man should have two pockets to use as occasion demands. In one pocket 'For my sake the world was created,' in the other 'I am dust and ashes.'" For Hasidism, touch-stones of reality are a living witness and not mere words, not *saying* Torah but *being* Torah. After the death of Rabbi Moshe of Kobryn, one of his disciples was asked, "What was most important for your teacher?" The disciple thought a moment and replied, "Whatever he happened to be doing at the moment." Hasidism calls man not to be a saint or superhuman but to be "humanly holy" in the measure and manner of each one's personal resources. The uniqueness of each situation and each person is tirelessly stressed in Hasidism. Accused of altering the service by the congregation that he inherited from his father, one Hasidic master retorted, "I do exactly as my father did. He did not imitate, and I do not imitate!"

Particularly significant for the current constellation of religious philosophy and metaphysics in the Western world of thought is the Hasidic doctrine of *tzimtzum* — the metaphor of God's self-limitation in the act of creation that Hasidism takes over from the Lurian Kabbala. The highest reality of the Divine, as Hasidism reinterprets *tzimtzum*, is not Meister Eckhart's impersonal Godhead but the Absolute that makes itself into a Person in order to bring us into relationship with it. On account of his great love, says the Maggid of Mezritch, God limits his illuminating power in order that, like a father with his son, he may bring us stage by stage to where we may receive the revelation of the limitless original God. God's relation to the human being and to creation is a voluntary contraction that in no way limits his absoluteness.

Seen in its true dynamic and interactive character, *tzimtzum* stands as one of the greatest reformulations of the biblical understanding of creation. It shows God as at once separate from the world and humanity and yet in relationship to them, and in such a way that neither the separateness nor the togetherness can be shown as either temporally or logically prior. Creation, in this view, is the radical fact that establishes and reestablishes the world and behind which we cannot look to any primal state before creation or godhead before God. In our own existence, we can neither begin with our separate existence as persons and then deduce our relations to others nor begin with our relations with others and then deduce our uniqueness as separate persons. Rather, we must begin with both at once. In our relation to God, similarly, we cannot go back behind creation to some more basic fact. Yet this is just what the mystics, the theologians, and the metaphysicians constantly attempt to do. Through logical analysis of the relation between the human being and God, they separate out the two factors of separateness and relatedness and then make one or the other of them prior.

Paul Tillich rightly attacks the theists for making God a person beside other persons. But what he offers instead is no more satisfactory — a "Ground of Being" that satisfies our logic's desire for a reality undergirding man's relation with God and at the same time forgiving and accepting as only a personal God could do! Alfred North Whitehead and Charles Hartshorne, on the other hand, say that since God cannot logically be both absolute and relational, they prefer to sacrifice the Absolute in favor of an imperfectly actual God who attains completion only through dialectical interaction with the world. The Hasidic understanding of the relation of God and the world does not have to fall into these logical alternatives. It can bear paradox because it sticks to the concrete given of our existence in which the seemingly irreconcilable opposites produced by our analytical thought exist together as one whole.

Hasidism is only one of the reinterpretations of biblical Judaism. Biblical Judaism is the mother of both rabbinical Judaism and orthodox Christianity and, by the same token, the grandmother or great-grandmother of modern Judaism and modern Christianity. Despite the continuity of the name and people, it should not surprise us, therefore, that there is much in present-day Judaism that is farther from biblical Judaism than the teachings of Jesus, who stood within the living tradition of biblical and early rabbinic Judaism.

Idolatry does not arise from images of God but from taking any particular image to be God. Certainly the imagelessness of God has been a central emphasis in Judaism; yet there has been no lack of Talmudists, philosophers, and *halachists* who have wanted to fix God in one image or another. The problem is not whether the imageless God reveals himself, as he must if there is to be a relationship to him, but whether these revelations are taken as universal, objective attributes of God or as God's relationship to man in concrete situations, capable of being transformed and renewed in still other concrete situations. "You are my witnesses, saith the Lord," we read in Isaiah, and the Talmud adds, "If you are not my witnesses, then I am not the Lord." What is this but a reiteration of the covenantal relationship in which we witness for God by bringing every aspect of our lives into dialogue with him? But the Jehovah's Witnesses have objectified this "witness" into something that can be handed out in pamphlets, in memorized speeches, in phonograph records. Just such objectification takes place if one claims that the Jews *are* the "chosen people" in abstraction from the covenant — that dynamic of relationship and falling away from relationship that led Hosea to name his son *Lo-Ami*, "Not my People," when Israel had turned away from God.

To speak, as many Christians do, of Jesus being perfect as man and as showing a way of perfection that others can follow, has no meaning to me, perhaps because I gave up perfection as something desirable and attainable when I abandoned my mystical striving for spiritual self-sufficiency in favor of a life in and with the world. If we are going to talk about creation and history, we cannot talk about perfection; for there is no perfection in human existence, any more than there is, in my view, an innate sinfulness in man. There is only taking up a task with the resources that we have. Therefore, I do not pray with Jesus, "Lead us not into temptation," but rather that we may have the resources to bring the temptation into meaningful human dialogue or at least not to be overwhelmed by it. Every moment is a moment of temptation, as Jesus knew well, for every new moment is unique — a new reality that we must withstand, a new task that we have to face, or a new bit of concrete existence that must be brought into our lives and allowed to affect it.

I affirm the biblical covenant as a covenant of trust between God and a people, between God and every people, to be renewed in every age according to the cruel but real demands of that age. The biblical covenant is not the exclusive possession of modern Judaism any more than it is of modern Christianity. Jesus is, to me, one of the unique bearers of the covenant, as is Abraham, Job, Isaiah, and the Baal Shem Tov. He is not to me *the* unique bearer; for no one moment of history may do the work of all other moments: if it comes down to us in its uniqueness, it must be taken up into the uniqueness of this new historical hour. Jesus is not an image of God to me. The paradox of our being created in God's image lies in the fact that it is precisely God's imagelessness that is imitated and represented in the uniqueness of each new person. But Jesus *is* an image of the human to me — along with Job and Saint Francis, Socrates and Lao-tzu, the Buddha and Albert Camus. Even Jesus denials were a part of his faithfulness to the covenant, his direct dialogue with the Father, his concern for "the Kingdom." His "Take no thought for the morrow" is an unforgettable renewal of biblical *emunah*, as is that verse without whose commonsense wisdom and intimations of the morrow's grace I could hardly live from one day to the next: "Sufficient unto the day is the evil thereof." Jesus' life and his crucifixion are not, for me, the fulfillment of "prophecy," but a true incarnation of the "suffering servant," who has never long been absent — from Abraham to the "Job of Auschwitz."[1]

Part two

Religious Experience
and
Religious Communication

3

The Meeting of Religion and Experience

Walking is Zen. Sitting is Zen.

"What is all this talk of praying 'earnestly'!" the rabbi of Kobryn
called to his Hasidim. "Is there anything at all that one ought not
to do earnestly?"

IN RELIGION our whole being responds and is involved in the
response. We respond to what we perceive as "ultimate reality." But we do not know this ultimate reality by prior metaphysical or theological definition. We know it only as we enter
into dialogue with it, only as we meet it in and through the concrete situations of our lives. Therefore, it is not the "object" that
we meet that is ultimate but the reality of the meeting itself.

Religion is the way that one walks, a basic commitment in life
itself. It expresses itself, to be sure, in doctrinal forms such as
myth, creed, theology, and metaphysics, in practical forms such
as liturgy, ritual, prayer, and in social forms such as fellowships,
churches, sects, and denominations. For all that, we cannot reduce religion to any one of these expressions or even to all of
them taken together and their interrelations. The matrix of all of
these expressions is our ultimate meeting itself, and this is not in
itself directly expressible. What is more, the expressions of religion inevitably come loose from their mooring, become de-

tached and independent. When this happens, it is necessary to return to the original immediacy, to reestablish the ultimate meeting that creed, ritual, and social form no longer lead us back to.

Our approach to religion and human experience is then a dialogical one. I use the word *dialogue* here not in the sense of two people speaking, but in the sense of openness, directness, mutuality, and presentness. Dialogue means here a mutual knowing, a knowing in direct contact in contrast to a detached subject's knowledge of an object. It may arise in the dialogue between person and person, including the sharing that I have called "a dialogue of touchstones." But it may also arise in our meeting with any nonhuman reality, the sunset over the ocean, a ghost pine on Point Lobos, the cry of the loon, the grandeur of the mountains, and the aggravations of everyday toil. It also may come in that indirect dialogue we know as art — paintings, sculpture, poetry, dance, orchestral and chamber music.

Not all religion is dialogue, of course, and neither is all knowing or, for that matter, all human experience. In one sense, human experience includes just everything in a person's life, inner and outer, conscious and unconscious, waking reality, fantasy, or dream. In another, it may be limited to what is singled out from among the stream of happenings, that which has an impact and stands out for itself. When we say, "I had an experience," we mean just that: something surfaces from the general flux as an event in itself and does so precisely because it impinges on us in some way, whether through the feelings it arouses — pleasure, pain, joy, misery — or through the significance we attach to it, or through the awe or wonder that it evokes. Although we certainly are not consciously aware of all the experiences that happen to us, we can, nonetheless, say that experience is that which we become aware of.

One of the most puzzling difficulties in any attempt to arrive at a phenomenology of human experience is the subtle change in the meaning and emphasis of the term over the last century and a half. In a picaresque novel, say, one by Charles Dickens, *experience* means the external happenings in the life of Mr. Pickwick or David Copperfield. Today, experience is often thought of as essentially an internal matter. If one speaks of drug experiences, "the Jimi Hendrix experience," sex or love experiences, or even religious experience, one means primarily the experience of being "turned on." "I saw you last night and got that old feeling." If the song concludes, "That old feeling is still in my heart," that is as it should be; for, essentially, it is the feeling *within* me that I am concerned with, not what is *between* me and you The feeling may be so expansive that it seems to include us both, as in the song "Marie Elena": "A love like mine is great enough for two. To share this love is really all I ask of you." But a love that demands so little, and so much, is the love of one's own feelings that "Marie Elena" arouses and occasions, not a love *between* Marie Elena and me. If "altered states of consciousness" is substituted for love, the situation is in no way changed. My concern with the reality that I meet is at best incidental. Either it and the meeting with it are the mere occasions for my elevations and ecstasies or these altered states of consciousness are held to be the higher reality itself. Consciousness, and in particular "higher consciousness," has become for many the new, self-evident touchstone of reality.

A look at dreams may further illustrate our problem. Dreams are regarded by Freudians and Jungians alike as "within," the pure raw material of the unconscious. Yet if we look at dreams more closely, we shall see that this cannot possibly be the case. Researchers tell us that we "dream" all the time. But when I tell you that I had a dream last night, I am not referring to some activity that can be picked up through appropriate electrodes placed in my brain and connected with an encephalograph, but to a series of events that I remember precisely because their impact on me enabled me to lift them out of the general flow. In this sense, dreams are exactly the same as any other experience. We "have" the dream through remembering it and, perhaps in addition, writing it down and/or recounting it to others. But in that remembering, writing, and recounting, three other things are taking place. First, we cut the dream loose from the aura of less well-remembered "dream events" as well as from emotions and sensations that cling to it but cannot be communicated. By the same token, we give the dream a form, a *Gestalt*, that enables us to contemplate it as a whole in itself. Second, we transfer the dream from the peculiar logic of our sleeping world to the very different logic of our waking consciousness and, in so doing, shape and elaborate it. We also elaborate it through our own first thoughts and feelings about it *and*, equally importantly, through our anticipations of whom we might tell it to. If we tell it to our therapist, we are likely to find ourselves highlighting those aspects that fit his or her school of psychology, whether Freudian, Jungian, Adlerian, Gestalt, or whatever. Third, and most important of all, having set the dream over against us, thus having isolated, shaped, and elaborated and given it form as an independent opposite, we enter into dialogue with it. From now on, it becomes one of the realities that addresses us in the world, just as surely and as concretely as any so-called external happening.

From this illustration it should be clear that we cannot understand human experience either as merely external or internal or even as a sum of the two, with some part of each experience the one and some part the other. Experience in the truest sense is itself an event of the "between." It is our meeting with whatever accosts us in the situation in which we find ourselves, dragon, damsel, or dream. One of the things that makes it difficult to understand this, as we have said, is our habit of regarding experience as something that takes place inside ourselves. Another is the pseudo-objectification that arises from our identifying experience with experiential and experiential with science. The so-called empirical sciences do, indeed, have a foundation in our experience. Yet they become sciences precisely by abstracting from the concrete uniqueness of the experienced event and turning what is thus abstracted into data that can be set into relation to other data through placing them into categories of class, condition, cause, or field of operation and interaction.

If there are difficulties that attend any phenomenology of human experience, there are still greater difficulties that attend a phenomenology of religious experience. When William James wrote his great classic, *The Varieties of Religious Experience*, he presented with admirable openness a whole range of "religious experiences" from mysticism and drugs to saintliness and conversion. Though his conclusion was pragmatic ("Religion is real because it has real effects"), it was not yet subjective in the way that religious experience has since tended to become. Today a religious experience is less something that seizes one on one's way than it is an experience that one "has," often by willfully setting out to have it. This is so much the case that I am often inclined to jettison the term *religious experience* entirely in favor of *religious reality* or *religious event* or any other term that might help liberate us from the bondage of the new subjectivism.

Another, older problem in the phenomenology of religious experience arises from the tendency to regard religion as a special experience to be set alongside sensory experience, aesthetic experience, sexual experience, or the like. If we do that, we give up once for all the claim that religion has to do with human wholeness in favor of seeing religion as one special sphere of life, perhaps that of mystic ecstasy, higher consciousness, fervent devotion, contemplation, trance, or even, as some would hold today, schizophrenia! Religion then becomes relegated to special times and places — Easter Sunday and Yom Kippur, the church or synagogue. As the "upper story" of our lives, it then usually has less claim on our total response than an absorbing piece of theater or symphony orchestra concert, or even a very good dinner or an engrossing game of football. It becomes, indeed, with all its prescribed creeds and rituals, downright tedious and boring.

On the other hand, if we seek to make religion equal to the sum total of human experience, we have either robbed religion of its reality entirely or we have reduced it to John Dewey's common faith, a vague idealism superimposed upon experience as the "religious" dimension of everyday life. For the whole to be greater than the sum of its parts, that whole must have a wholeness that is integral to it. It must come together into a whole the way the various notes of a composition come together, when performed, to become a piano concerto or a string quartet. If religion is a way that we walk, then the whole of human life is included in it. Yet that life comes to wholeness not additively or by abstraction but only in the upsurging of events in which all the moments of the past are caught up into the present and given new reality by it. Such an event could be an hour of prayer at a time of great need — when we are facing death or are facing the death of loved ones. Or it could be a moment of breathtaking awe before a waterfall or in the midst of a raging storm at sea. Or it could be an action in which we gather together all the past meanings of our life in one great hour of devotion or sacrifice. In all cases, it is an event in which we attain selflessness not by giving up the self, as the ascetics suggest that we do, but by the totality of our response. In such a totality we are taken out of ourselves, called out by something to which we respond so fully and spontaneously that our self is neither our aim nor our concern but only the self-understood and self-evident ground of our responding.

To understand religion in this sense, we must unify our phenomenology of human experience and our phenomenology of religion into a phenomenology of the *meeting* of religion and experience. Here we risk confusion because we have already defined experience as, in one sense, itself a product of meeting. It is also the springboard and base for future meetings. We go out from our present experience to meet the new that befalls us. We bring our experience with us into what we meet. We meet that experience itself in our reflections on it and our concern with it — as in holding in our mind a dream or a personal exchange that has touched our heart, not analyzing it but letting it speak to us and letting ourselves answer this address.

We can clear up our confusion further if we recognize that *religion* is often treated as being the external forms that seem to the observer to make up religion — ritual, organization, creed — and experience is often seen as the subjective aspect of our existence — our feelings, our consciousness, or even our unique participation in an event common to ourselves and others. Looked at in this way, we could then speak of the meeting of religion and experience as a way of pointing to the reality of the between that cannot be caught in the objective forms of religion or the subjective forms of experience. Only in this way, perhaps, can we point ourselves back — and forward — to that "ultimate response to what is encountered as ultimate" that we have tentatively defined as religion.

Yet we shall not be satisfied with approaching religion through a double negative — *not* objective and *not* subjective — or even by defining religion as a dialogical reality that the objective expressions and the subjective experiences are merely the byproducts of and accompaniments to. We shall want, instead, to speak of this dialogical reality itself and in its own terms, as an event of meeting that comes to light *before* our abstractions into external and internal, objective and subjective, thought and feeling, and the like. To do this we must turn to that neglected reality that gives this book its title — the *Human Way*, or, to use my Latin original, the *via humana*.

4

The *Via Humana*

Rabbi Leib, the son of Sarah, said, "I did not go to the Maggid of Mezritch to hear him say Torah, but to see how he unlaces his felt shoes and laces them up again."

It is written: "And ye shall be holy men unto Me."
The rabbi of Kotzk explained: "Ye shall be holy unto me, but as men, ye shall be humanly holy unto me."[1]

I N THE CHAPTER on religious symbolism in *Touchstones of Reality*, I coin the term the *via humana* to set in contrast with the two traditional approaches — the *via positiva*, which describes the attributes of God, and the *via negativa*, which emphasizes the utter unknowability of God and speaks only of what God is not:

The importance of touchstones of reality as an approach is that it does not claim to be the absolute truth, but it also does not abandon us to some completely subjective relativism. It witnesses to as much reality as we can witness to at that moment. In opposition to both the *via negativa* and the *via positiva*, therefore, I would make bold to call touchstones of reality the *via humana*. Only through it can we keep close to the concrete reality, without pursuing theology at the expenses of the fully human or humanism at the expense of closing man off from the nameless reality that he meets in his meeting with everyday life (232 f.).

In using *The Human Way,* or the *via humana,* as the title of this book, I am taking it out of the context of theology and religious symbolism and giving it the broader meaning of the dialogical approach to religion and human experience — the way that we walk in the concrete situations of our existence. If we wish to put this in a theological context, we might speak of theology as biography, or "dialography" (see p. 67), theology as event. But to do so already changes radically the traditional meaning of theology. It no longer rests upon a set of traditional beliefs and presuppositions nor even upon a traditional interpretation of "sacred history" and biblical events. Rather it is the event itself that again and again gives rise to religious meaning, and only out of that meaning, apprehended in our own history and the history of past generations that we have made present to ourselves, do religious symbols and theological interpretations arise. For this reason, I have found it difficult to go along with those of my friends who call for a return to theology as an antidote to the excessive naturalism and restrictive "humanism" of the recent past. I believe in a larger humanism that is defined not by negation of transcendent reality but precisely by the fact that it negates nothing and is open to the concrete and unique, even if it should manifest itself, as William James puts it, "in the very dirt of private fact."

With these cautions in mind, what can we say of *theology as event*? First, that it is much more modest than traditional theology and metaphysics in that it claims to know nothing about what God is "in Himself." This is not such a great sacrifice as it might at first appear if one holds, as I do, that the philosopher does not have access to absolute Truth but only a relation to truth and the revelations of which the theologian speaks do not put us in firm possession of the "essence" of God but speak to us in and out of particular historical situations.

On my desk is a colleague's invitation to a *chanukkat habayit,* a dedication of a new household. As I reflect on the meaning of the word *chanukah*, almost lost sight of in the lighting of candles and cooking of lotkes at the Jewish festival by that name, I am struck by the fact that it was a celebration *millenia afterwards* of the rededication of a profaned temple that itself no longer exists and has not existed for two thousand years! David was forbidden to build himself a temple but had only the wandering ark. When King Solomon built his temple, one of the wonders of the ancient world, it signaled the beginning of the deterioration of biblical Judaism from the covenant with God that the people entered into with their whole personal and social existence to the dualism in which God was served only with holy rites — incense, ritual, and sacrifice — and no longer with everyday life. It is against just this dualism that the prophets of the Hebrew Bible inveighed — one after the other in each historical situation. Nonetheless, for the millenium and more that the First and Second Temple lasted, the temple was the sacral center of religious life in the land. People went up to it from all over the land once a year, bringing their offerings, coming to be forgiven, purified, reconciled, atoned. When the Maccabees drove the idolatrous vestments of Hellenistic culture out of the temple, they felt that they were restoring the holiness that dwelled in the temple. Yet in modern Judaism the historical event stands out far beyond the original significance of the rewedding of sacred act and sacred place. The destruction of the temple is mourned, to be sure, on the ninth of Av. Yet it is mourned not as the ritual center of Judaism but as the symbol of an event, the Diaspora, the great scattering, the millenia of exile that separated the people from their religious covenant, from the land, and from one another.

We can also say of theology as event that it makes a staggering claim, namely, that it is in our lives that we apprehend the divine — not through sacred times and places and rituals alone but in the everyday happening, "the days of our years." Christianity says this in the most dramatic way of all — that God has become incarnated in a man like ourselves, that he has suffered and died and been resurrected, and that our access to the divine is through the celebration, the creative remembering, of just those events. But Judaism says it too; for Judaism is a religion of events, of touchstones of reality, and each of its great holidays is a celebration of events. The Ten Commandments do not begin with the proclamation of God as Cosmic King or even Creator but as Historical Redeemer:

> Rabbi Bunam was asked: "It is written: 'I am the Lord thy God, who brought thee out of the land of Egypt.' Why does it not read: 'I am the Lord thy God, who created heaven and earth'?"
> Rabbi Bunam expounded: "'Heaven and earth!' Then man might have said: 'Heaven — that is too much for me.' So God said to man: 'I am the one who fished you out of the mud. Now you come here and listen to me!'"[2]

The Book of Deuteronomy reaffirms the biblical covenant by demanding that the individual and the people love God with all their heart, soul, and might. This, as Jesus rightly said, implies and includes the famous injunction in Leviticus, to "love your neighbor as yourself," that is to deal lovingly with the person with whom you have to do as one equal to yourself. Instead of the revelation being safeguarded by removing it to an impossible transcendence, what is stressed is the reality of present dialogue — "It is not our fathers but we who stand on Mount Sinai to receive the covenant" — and the immediacy of the demand God places on man:

> This commandment which I command you this day is not too hard for you, neither is it far off. It is not in heaven, that you should say, "Who will go up for us to heaven and bring it to us, that we may hear it and do it?" ... But the word is very near you; it is in your mouth and in your heart, so that you can do it.
>
> (Deut. 30:11-14)

The famous response of the Israelites to Moses when he gave them the Torah, the covenant, says the same thing even more dramatically: *Na'aseh v'nishmah*: "We shall do and we shall hear" — out of our doing itself. The revelation is not given to us before history but in the midst of history, and it is in our dialogue with history, with the events great and small that make up our lives, that we learn what it is that we are commanded to do. This applies to the everyday as much as to the great crises in history.

An important part of most religions is prayer, but prayer is also an event and issues into events. For the Hasidim, God Himself is prayer, but that is only true when true praying *happens* as a dialogical reality. "Nicholas was born in answer to prayer," says Benjamin Britten's *St. Nicholas Cantata*. This does not mean, as we might think, that our prayers are "answered" in the sense that we are given what we pray for. The people did not know who Nicholas was until he was in their midst. Yet praying itself is a powerful event, and out of prayer the reality between God and man is changed.

To speak of religion as event in no way means to reduce religion to ethics. It means only that our total existence is involved in religion, that it is *not* some sacred upper story that has nothing to do with the rest of our lives. The Sermon on the Mount is no doubt a compilation from different traditional texts, but it is also without doubt built from teachings that Jesus gave or was reported to give to the people to whom he spoke as he walked about in Palestine. That some people have regarded this teaching as unrealistic or too idealistic in no wise detracts from its concern with the whole of human existence. "If the salt hath lost its savor, wherewith shall it be salted?" If the human being has lost what makes him or her truly human, there is no way to replace this with something else such as power or success or prestige. Even if it is, as Reinhold Niebuhr claimed, "an impossible ideal," it is still relevant. It still brings us into judgment because it sets a direction for our movement.

One of my students was once profoundly troubled because, in teaching the Sermon on the Mount, I raised the question of whether the students thought Jesus' injunction to turn the other cheek and walk the second mile was in accord with human nature as we are coming to understand it from modern psychology. She was not troubled because this is a troublesome question, as it is indeed, but because she had never thought of the Sermon on the Mount as a teaching that *she* might follow. For her it was only a part of the image of Christ's perfection! When Jesus ceases to be an image of the human and becomes instead an image of the divine, the *way* in which our existence is involved, if we are

Christians, is likely radically to change, though not the fact of that involvement.

A similar development takes place in Buddhism. Whether or not Gautama actually went through the noble Eightfold Path himself before attaining enlightenment, it seems certain that he or some of his disciples devised the Eightfold Path —right views, right resolution, right speech, right action, right livelihood, right will, right mindfulness, and right meditation — as a mnemonic guide to others who are following the path to enlightenment and Nirvana. It is unthinkable that this Path was taught simply as an adornment to the image of the Buddha's perfection. Later when the Buddha came to be worshiped, the marks of perfection were quite other, physical ones, or they were stories of his sacrifice of himself in previous births, as in the Jatatka Tales. But even when Mahayana Buddhism developed the concepts of Buddhahood, Transcendent Wisdom, and salvation through the grace of the Bodhisattva, none of these implied a moving of religion from the ground of existence to that of a timeless ideal or spiritual upper story. The whole existence was still claimed, though in a radically different way.

This is equally evident in Taoism and Confucianism. Whether the *Tao Te-Ching* be translated as "The Canon of Reason and Virtue" or as "The Way of Life," it is still manifestly a way that a person walks. It is not an isolated ethic; for its central concern is with the Tao that rounds the way of heaven and earth and is the way of the person. At first glance the Analects of Confucius might appear more as pure ethics, or even etiquette, yet its link with the heaven that "knew" Confucius when no one else knew him, is as unmistakable as its concern with the whole of human life. In Hinduism the ethical occasionally appears like a stage one must attain or go through to reach higher spiritual paths. Yet the four yogas, or *margas*, of discrimination, action, devotion, and meditation themselves constitute a total way of life.

Basic to the Hebrew Bible, as to the Vedanta's conception of *Nirguna* Brahman and Lao-tzu's understanding of the Tao, is that "God" is imageless. The *via negativa* of the mystics stresses again and again our inability to describe or conceptualize the God whom we can somehow meet in our lives. Yet the Bible speaks of our being created in God's image. If we place these two thoughts together, we arrive at the paradox that we are created in the image of the imageless God. If we hold the tension of this paradox and even deepen it, we shall deepen our understanding of the *via humana*. All religions and philosophies have come to a blank wall in trying to explain the relation of Being to Becoming, the One to the Many, the Uncreated Creator to the Creation, Eternity to Time. Yet the paradox we are faced with goes even beyond this problem, insuperable as it is. For we are asking how it is possible that Eternity has to do with us, human beings, mortals, living and dying in our time-bound, culture-conditioned, geographically and economically constricted lives. We are not asking for an answer in any metaphysical sense but rather for the credibility of a claim — the claim that it is not by leaving the perishable for the constant, transiency for permanency that we make contact with the Eternal, but through the events of our changing, vacillating existence. In contrast to the old metaphysics, like that of Plato, we do not seek an ideal world above the moving images of time. Neither do we seek, like the new metaphysics of Martin Heidegger, for a Being or Truth that is to be revealed, or "unconcealed," in the phenomena of time. We seek rather for the reality of mutual contact, a happening that becomes for us a witness and for which we can ourselves witness — a touchstone of reality.

There are two approaches to human existence and meaning that I have developed independently of each other — that of the *image of man* or the *human image*, and that of *touchstones of reality*. To understand the *via humana* in greater depth, I must now try to grasp the interrelationship of these two approaches. They are not synonymous, yet both are ways of "meeting the nameless Meeter," both claim that "meaning is accessible in the lived concrete." As such, both are ways of speaking of the central biblical paradox that we are created in the image of an imageless God whom we cannot define or describe, imitate, or model ourselves after yet can relate to, meet, "know" in the direct, unmediated knowing of mutual contact in the events of our lives. To plumb this paradox is not an excursus in biblical theology; for essentially the same claim stands behind all religion. All religion is founded on the basic trust that this world is not a place in which we are hopelessly lost, that evil or illusory as the world may be, and sinful or ignorant as we are, there is a way, a path, that leads from darkness to light, from lostness to salvation, from evil to redemption.

To say that we were created in God's image confers a meaning and dignity on us that seems to contrast oddly with the fragility, instability, and complexity of our existence. It repeats the Psalmist's cry: "When I behold the heavens, the work of your hands, the sun and the stars that thou has placed there, what is man that you think of him and the son of man that you keep watch on him? Yet you have placed him just a little lower than God." Pascal experienced the terror before the infinity of the stars and the silent spaces in between them. Yet he could also affirm the human being as a finite middle between the infinite and the infinitesimal: not everything but also not nothing. Modern man sees only the terrifying vision of infinity, "the heartless voids and immensities that threaten us from behind with the thought of annihilation when beholding the white depths of the milky way" (Melville).

> This August night in a rift of cloud
> Antares reddens,
> Great one,
> Lord among lost kingdoms

wrote the American poet Robinson Jeffers in his long poem, "Night." (In high school, I was so struck by its philosophy and haunting beauty that I committed it to memory.)

> But to you, O night, what?
> Not a spark,
> Not a flicker of a spark,
> Dim coals from a sandpit
> The bedouins wandered from at dawn.

For us to reaffirm that we are created in God's image means to stand our ground before an infinity that we can neither encompass nor comprehend. It means to enclose the awful silence of the spaces between the stars in a renewed and deepened existential trust.

This trust will fail us if we are content to leave our affirmation in the form of some abstract essence of "human nature" — "that of God in every man," "a spark of the divine," "man's essential goodness." The real power of the creation in God's image is that somehow we can imitate God's ways in relation to us, that we can become like the Eternal that we can only meet in the dimension of time. To do this we need not shed our mortal clothes as impediments but live a truly human life, authenticate our humanity as persons called to become what each of us, in our created uniqueness, can become. What is actual and what is potential must become transfigured by a direction through which our divine essence can permeate our existence. It is my concern for this direction that led me to occupy myself with the "human image" over a span of a quarter of a century.

Whatever may be the case with religion, the religious person has always been aware of the central importance of our images of true human existence. This is because the religious life is not in the first instance affirmation of a creed nor is it philosophy or gnosis — an attempt to know *about* the world or God — but a way that the human person walks *with* God, a flowing with the Tao, a discovery of "the action that is in inaction, the inaction that is in action." For the religious person, it is not enough to have a philosophy of life: one must live one's philosophy. "Not to say Torah but to be Torah" — this is the existential demand that all religion ultimately places on us. Philosophies of religion are ultimately meaningless abstractions if we divorce them from the living Buddha, Lao-tzu, Confucius, Jesus, Mohammed, Moses, St. Francis, and the Baal-Shem-Tov. Swami Prahavananda and Christopher Isherwood claim in their introduction to the *Bhagavad-Gita*, the Hindu "Song of God," that it does not matter whether Christ or Krishna really lived because we have their teachings and they are universal. In so doing they miss the central reality from which all religious teachings spring and to which they again and again point back: the image of the human. The historical Krishna is not so important to Hinduism as the historical Jesus is to Christianity. But even so a one-time historical human image stands behind the avatar.

Touchstones of reality point to a "narrow ridge" between an objective reality existing outside of us and a subjective truth minus mutual contact with real otherness. Like our images of the human, touchstones of reality are the way in which the past is brought into the present and made present anew. Both touchstones of reality and the image of the human are a product of meeting and a way of entering new meetings. Both provide a link between the past and the present without fixing the present in the past. Both abjure timeless absolutes, world views, and the security of smooth continuity. The link between the imageless God and the human image becomes particularly concrete in touchstones of reality; for our touchstones of reality are themselves the bond between the absolute and the particular, the embodiment of symbol in the lived life of actual persons.

The meaning of the religious symbol is found not in its universality but in the fact that it points to a concrete event that witnesses just as it is, in all its concreteness, transitoriness, and uniqueness, to the relation with the Absolute. The symbol becomes abstract, to be sure, when it is detached from a concrete event, when "the finger pointing at the moon is taken for the moon itself." When that happens, the symbol obstructs our meeting with God; for it is deprived of its real, concrete meaning in favor of the all-meaning of the universal and the spiritual. This all-meaning is always only a substitute for the meaning apprehended in the concrete.

We do not have to put aside particularity and the reality of time, therefore, to find our touchstones of reality; for they are an integral part of the *via humana*: they have to do with the full seriousness of the moment. The fact that this moment will not come again does not mean it is unreal or illusory. On the contrary, it is the one thing that is given us to make real. Because the *via humana* means the covenant between the Absolute and the concrete, the meaning of the religious symbol is not independent of lived human life in all its concreteness. Not only does this lived concreteness originally produce the symbol, but only this can renew its meaning for those who have inherited it and save it from becoming merely spiritual and not truly existential.

The marriage of the prophet Hosea with a "woman of whorishness," that is to say a woman whose heart inclines to whoredom, represents the marriage between YHVH and this land, his love which his wife has betrayed represents YHVH's love which Israel has betrayed, his separation from the faithless one the divine separation, his mercy on her God's mercy.[3]

If the religious symbol is grounded in such a concrete and particular event, how then does it carry over from that moment of history to this? It can only do that if it is renewed again in all concreteness in another moment of lived history to which it speaks. William Blake bases his poem-preface to "Milton" on the historical fact of Jesus walking in Jerusalem: "And did those feet in ancient time," but he transposes the setting immediately to contemporary England: "Walk upon England's mountains green?" And he ends by demanding that the ancient event be real in the present, "Among these dark Satanic Mills":

> I will not cease from Mental Fight,
> Nor shall my Sword sleep in my hand
> Till we have built Jerusalem
> In England's green and pleasant Land.

Touchstones of reality are particularly helpful in understanding the paradox of religious symbolism. All symbols need to be interpreted, yet much of concrete reality is lost in conceptualizing. There is a necessary dialectic between symbol and interpretation, or better between one type of symbol and another — poetry and philosophy, religion and metaphysics, myth and concept. There is a strong modern tendency to reduce religion to symbolism in which the symbol does not derive from meeting with the other or the divine but is merely the imaginative projection of human ideals and aspirations or manifestations of the psyche or of the collective unconscious. This is true not only of Freud but also of Fromm and Jung and popular culture in general. Metaphysical analogies, including religious symbols, are actually, as Dorothy Emmett has pointed out, analogies between relationships rather than between a familiar object and an unfamiliar one. To say, "The Lord is my shepherd," is not to liken the divine in itself to a shepherd in himself but our relationship to the divine, in one of its aspects, to the relationship of a good shepherd to the sheep he cares for.

A symbol may point back to or obstruct the nonsymbolic religious reality that gave rise to it. Touchstones of reality are less in danger of false objectification than ordinary religious symbols because they are less static and visual, more dynamic and two-sided. Touchstones of reality imply a radical reversal of the idealist and mystical view that sees the symbol as the concrete manifestation of some universal. The meaning of the symbol is found rather in its pointing to a concrete event that witnesses in all its transistoriness and uniqueness to our relationship with the Absolute. The legend of the parting of the Red Sea is a myth that arose in response to a particular, wonder-full moment of history. Freedom is the symbol of the Passover, the liberation of the Israelite slaves from Egypt, not the Passover the symbol of freedom, as some liberal rabbis have suggested. This was fully understood by the black slaves in America when the spiritual, "Go down Moses," arose in response to another concrete historical situation, as it was by Albert Camus when he wrote in *The Rebel*, "Nothing justifies the assertion that these principles have existed eternally.... But they do exist, in the very period in which we exist. With us, and throughout all history, they deny servitude, falsehood, and terror." Touchstones of reality have to do with the full seriousness of the unique moment, and only lived human life in all concreteness can renew the meaning of a symbol.

"All symbols are ever in danger of becoming spiritual and not binding images," writes Martin Buber. "Only through the man who devotes himself is the original power saved for further present existence." Buber does not mean the one who devotes oneself to the symbol the way a theologian might, interpreting and unfolding. He means the one who devotes oneself to the hour, who involves one's whole being in one's response to its claim. The life of such a one, one's nonsymbolic meeting with the people and things that confront one, may ultimately, indeed, be the truest and most meaningful symbol of our relationship to the divine. If the highest manifestation of the religious symbol is a human life lived in relation to the Absolute, this relationship is possible even when there is neither image nor symbol of God but only the address that we perceive and the demand to which we respond in our meeting with the everyday.

Our age is dominated, perhaps more than any before, by a dualism in which people live in one world and have their ideals and symbols in another. Our alternatives seem increasingly to be reality divested of symbols or symbols divested of reality. In such an age, the prerequisite to an image of the imageless God may be the rediscovery in our lives of an image of the human: an image of authentic human existence that stands its ground and faithfully encounters even the absurd. Religious witnesses are renewed when a situation or event speaks so powerfully that a John Woolman can suddenly hear in the American wilderness the teaching of George Fox, not as a doctrine to be preached but in his whole life — in his relations to the Indians and the black slaves and his fellow Quakers.

For the *via humana* the only truth that we can hope to possess is a human one. To say this implies no degradation of truth or even relativization. It does imply a humanization of truth, one that robs it of its false claim to literalness, dogma, and absoluteness. We cannot possess the Absolute but we can stand in relation to it, and our human truth is the product of that relation. Meaning, to the *via humana*, does not lie in any *Weltanschauung*, or world view, but in existential trust. This trust is not a trust that something is the case nor is it any evolutionary process, however attractive that view is to us moderns. Touchstones of reality and the dialogue of touchstones in which we share, encounter, and make our own the touchstones of others are our ultimate source of knowledge. We cannot possess even human truth as a secure continuity, but we can have relationship with it. We can allow it to be the finger pointing at the moon, or the way in which the Maggid laces and unlaces his felt shoes. Important as analytical thought, logic, empirical verification, and the resemblance of the future to the past are, the ultimate criterion of truth is the renewal of our former truth by bringing into each new and unique situation the touchstones of reality that have remained present to us.

From this standpoint, the conscious and verbal affirmation of the existence of God is less important than our deeply rooted human attitude or life-stance. Martin Buber wrote me that I should not call Albert Camus an atheist but one of those philosophers who destroy the images of God that no longer do justice to Him in order that the religious person may set out across the darkness to a new meeting with the nameless Meeter. Camus told R. W. B. Lewis that he would not mind being called religious in Buber's sense of the I-Thou relationship. Both Camus and Buber, the "atheist" and the theist, are paradigms of that human image that I call the Modern Job — one who trusts and contends within the Dialogue with the Absurd.

We do not have to have a "religion" to be human, but we do have to have touchstones of reality. I do not believe any person lives without some sort of touchstone, but a great many people do live without formal religion. Anyone who says that these people do not have ethical concerns or spiritual qualities is mistaken. I am more concerned with basic attitudes than with belief, with religious reality than with religion. Every religion perhaps originates in and points to religious reality, but it also often obstructs it. Even the religious communities in which we meet and confirm one another at times also obstruct the immediacy from which our touchstones spring and to which they have the power to point back.

The oneness of God, to me at least, is the renewed meeting with the ever-unique and the ever-particular. It is not some type of superabstraction above time and space. Many people feel that we have to choose between an exclusivist truth and a hopeless relativism. I feel, in contrast to *both* positions, that the reality of pluralism must be the starting point of any serious modern faith. We should give up looking for the one true religion and consider our religious commitments as unique relationships to a truth that we cannot possess. We live our lives in a movement between immediacy and objectification. What matters is not the one or the other taken by itself but the spirit that leads us from the one to the other and back again.

The Hebrew Bible speaks of God hiding his face. This means, in our terms, that we can no longer find a touchstone of reality, that we can no longer find a meaning, a contact. There are periods in history, such as the present, when the existential trust that underlies the courage to respond no longer seems possible, when the meeting with present reality in the everyday is lost in a welter of mistrust — psychological, political, social, even existential. The fact that we have a ground to stand on means nothing if we cannot use that ground to go out to meet a genuine other. The Job of Auschwitz had to face a reality that is by its very nature unfaceable. *The Diary of Anne Frank* can move millions, but the extermination of six million to eleven million unique persons exceeds our capacity to understand or even imagine. We live in the era of Auschwitz, Hiroshima, Vietnam, Biafra and Kampuchea — an era in which the social cement that held society together has been dissolved and the most ordinary social confidence is no longer present. We could not imagine in advance that people would systematically turn other persons into cakes of soap or irradiate people in such a way that they would die on the spot or slowly and horribly over a great many years. Yet now that this has happened, reality creates possibility, and the unthinkable is no longer unthinkable.

In my book, *To Deny Our Nothingness*, I have spoken of a Dialogue with the Absurd, implying that it is sometimes possible, without making the absurd anything other than absurd, to enter into dialogue with it, to find meaning in this dialogue. But this Dialogue with the Absurd does not in any way mean that the inconceivable horror that it has been our fate to witness and live through is anything other than just that. Any view which enables us to be comfortable with the destruction and endless suffering of countless of our contemporaries is surely a deception.

If the Modern Job, the Job of Auschwitz, nonetheless remains in dialogue with God, or, like Camus' hero Doctor Rieux in *The Plague*, in dialogue with the absurd, it is not an affirmation that really everything is for the best. It is existential trust that just in this terrible world and here only is reality. Rather than leave this world of "illusion" for some supposed oneness with the cosmic All or the God within, it is better to stand one's ground and contend as long as one has life and breath with which to contend.

5

Legend, Myth, and Tale; Religion and Literature

> A rabbi, whose grandfather had been a disciple of the Baal Shem,
> was asked to tell a story. "A story," he said, "must be told in such a
> way that it constitutes help in itself." And he told: "My grandfather
> was lame. Once they asked him to tell a story about his teacher.
> And he related how the holy Baal Shem used to hop and dance
> while he prayed. My grandfather rose as he spoke, and he was so
> swept away by his story that he himself began to hop and dance to
> show how the master had done. From that hour on he was cured
> of his lameness. That's the way to tell a story!"[1]

IF THE MATRIX of religion is the event that gives rise to the touchstone of reality, then we may expect to find in legend, myth,
and tale as faithful and full an expression of religious reality
as in creed, ritual, and social group. This presupposes, of course,
that legends, myths, and tales are not illustrations of preexisting
abstract ideas but that ideas, on the contrary, are monological
and static abstractions from the dramatic, dialogical reality of
the event, some part of which is still preserved in legend, myth,
and tale.

The most concrete and dramatic form of the religious symbol
is the myth. Or perhaps it would be more accurate to say that
one of the first abstractions from myth is the symbol. C. G. Jung
and Ananda K. Coomaraswamy tend to see the myth as an

embodiment in different forms and cultures of a perennial reality, the psychological process whereby integration of the personality is achieved and the divine Self realized within the personal unconscious or the spiritual process whereby the one becomes the many and the many returns unto the one. Ernst Cassirer's understanding of myth, in contrast, leaves room for the concrete, particular event and the dialogue with it; and his distinction between *discursive* and *mythical thinking* offers us an important insight into the place of the myth in the dialogue of touchstones that constitutes much of religious tradition.

Discursive thinking denotes what has already been noticed. It classifies into groups and synthesizes parts into a whole. It does not contemplate a particular case but instead gives it a fixed intellectual meaning and definite character by linking it with other cases into a general framework of knowledge. The particular is never important in itself but only in terms of its relation to this framework. An even, grey light illumines the whole series of linked happenings. Mythical thinking, in contrast, is not concerned with relating data but with a sudden intuition, an immediate experience in which it comes to rest. It is like a strong white light that focuses on a single event in such a way that everything else is left in darkness. "The immediate content ... so fills his consciousness that nothing else can exist beside and apart from it." This content "is not merely viewed and contemplated, but overcomes a man in sheer immediacy."[2] For all this, there is a telltale residue of German philosophical idealism in Cassirer that leads him to see the historical fact as meaningful only as a member of a course of events or a teleological nexus and not in its particularity and uniqueness, as one would suppose from the rest of his thought on myth.

Henri Frankfort's treatment of myth builds on that of Cassirer but is more dialogical than is Cassirer's. Making use of Buber's distinction between the I-Thou and I-It relations, in itself quite close to Cassirer's contrast between mythical and discursive thinking, Frankfort identifies myth with the dynamically reciprocal I-Thou relationship in which every faculty of the human being is involved. He recognizes, moreover, the unique and unpredictable character of the Thou — "a presence known only insofar as it reveals itself."

> "Thou" is not contemplated with intellectual detachment; it is experienced as life confronting life.... The whole man confronts a living "Thou" in nature; and the whole man — emotional and imaginative as well as intellectual — gives expression to the experience.

Frankfort recognizes that myth arises not only in connection with humanity's relation to nature, the cosmos, and the change of the seasons, but also in our relation to a transcendent God in the course of history. But when he speaks of the will of God, the chosen people, and the Kingdom of God as "myths," he tends to remove from history the concreteness that is of its very essence.

> The doctrine of a single, unconditioned, transcendent God ... postulated a metaphysical significance for history and for man's actions.... In transcending the Near Eastern myths of immanent godhead, they [the Hebrews] created ... the new myth of the will of God. It remained for the Greeks, with their peculiar *intellectual* courage, to discover a form of speculative thought in which myth was entirely overcome.[3]

It appears that, even for Frankfort, myth is primarily important as a form of thought rather than as an embodiment of concrete events.

We must turn to Martin Buber for a thoroughly dialogical and consistently concrete understanding of myth. Although in his early thinking Buber also saw myth as a particular manifestation of a universal mystical reality, by 1907 he already distinguished between the *pure myth* in which there is variety without differentiation and the *legend* in which the subject is divided and God and the hero or saint stand opposed to one another as I and Thou. In 1921 Buber elaborated this concept into a distinction between myth, saga, and legend. *Myth* is the expression of a world in which the divine and the human live next to and in one another; *saga* is the expression of a world in which they are no longer intertwined and man already begins to sense with a shudder what is over against him; *legend* expresses a world in which the separation is completed, but now a dialogue and interchange takes place from sphere to sphere and it is of this that the myth tells. True history must include just that concreteness and uniqueness that Cassirer attributes to mythical thinking; for real history contains at its core the memory of the concrete and particular meeting between I and Thou. "I hold myth to be indispensable," writes Buber, "but I do not hold it to be central.... Myth must verify itself in man and not man in myth. What is wrong is not the mythicization of reality which brings the inexpressible to speech, but the gnosticizing of myth which tears it out of the ground of history and biography in which it took root." Buber refuses the alternatives of factual history or universal and timeless myth and proclaims the history that gives rise to myth, the myth that remembers history:

> What is preserved for us here is to be regarded not as the "historization" of a myth or a cult drama, nor is it to be explained as the transposition of something originally beyond time into historical time: a great history-faith does not come into the world through interpretation of the extra-historical as historical, but by receiving an occurrence experienced as a "wonder," that is as an event which cannot be grasped except as an act of God.[4]

The *saga* is the direct and unique expression of the reporter's knowledge of an event. Rather, this knowledge is itself a legendary one, representing (through the organic work of mythicizing memory) the believed-in action of God in dialogue with a person or people. It is not fantasy that is active here but memory — that believing memory of the souls and generations of early times that arises without arbitrary action from the impulse of an extraordinary event. Even the myth that seems most fantastic of all is created around the kernel of the organically shaping memory. "Here, unlike the concept familiar in the science of religion, myth is nothing other than the report by ardent enthusiasts of that which has befallen them. Here history cannot be dissevered from the historical wonder; but the experience which has been transmitted to us, the experience of event as wonder, is itself great history and must be understood out of the element of history."

This same combination of history, event, and wonder recurs in Buber's mature retelling of Hasidic tales in which he reconstructed the pure event in the form of the legendary anecdote.

> They are called anecdotes because each of them communicates an event complete in itself, and legendary because at the base of them lies the stammering of inspired witnesses who witnessed to what befell them, to what they comprehended as well as to what was incomprehensible to them; for the legitimately inspired has an honest memory that can nonetheless outstrip all imagination.[5]

This approach to event does not dismiss the comparative aspects of the history of religion, but leaves room for uniqueness. "Irrespective of the importance of the typological view of phenomena in the history of the spirit, the latter, just because it is history, also contains the atypical, the unique in the most precise sense." This concern with uniqueness is a natural corollary of the bond between the Absolute and the concrete, the particular. From this standpoint, legend, myth, and tale point us back to the concrete, unique event from which they took their rise. The mythical element may also, of course, become so strong that the kernel of historical memory tends to be obscured. Then, where event and memory cease to rule, myth replaces them by a timeless image.

Some myths contain within themselves the nexus of a historical event experienced by a group or by an individual; many have lost their historical character and contain only the symbolic expression of a universal experience of man. Even in the latter case, countless concrete meetings of I and Thou have attained symbolic expression in the relatively abstract form. The universality and profundity of these myths lie in the fact that they are products of actual human experience and tell us something about the structure of human reality that nothing else can. The myth of the Garden of Eden is universal, not as a timeless truth arising from somewhere beyond concrete human existence, but rather as something that happens anew to every human being.

"The point of mythology," writes Harry M. Buck, "is that man does not act objectively toward the world; he encounters it and participates in it. Myth is not merely a story told, but a reality lived, a sanction for a way of life and a pattern for worship." The type of myth that Buck has in mind is what we have called universal — one in which the universality grows out of the existential:

> The myth is not meaningful or true because it contains elements of history, but because it places certain events — whether or not items of chronological history — into a scheme which possesses an existential character. That scheme is an expression of man's view of himself.[6]

The first criterion for a religious myth, according to Buck, is its involvement with metahistorical time. In this he follows Mircea Eliade, who succeeded our teacher Joachim Wach to the chair of History of Religion at the University of Chicago. Like Eliade, Buck sees the myth as paradigmatic, "an expression of a classical archetype and itself the archetype for future thought and action." Though this emphasis on archetypes has a Jungian slant that Eliade shares, for Eliade and Buck the importance of true myth is that it points us back to the primordial time that Eliade calls *in illo tempore*. From this perspective "the Passover is not a true myth, because it does have a point of origin in historical time and not *in illo tempore*; but it fulfills many of the same functions as a myth." The Passover, indeed, is what Buber calls a saga, the product of the organically shaping memory that is still faithful to a kernel of historical event.

In *Cosmos and History* Mircea Eliade sets in opposition the archetypal, cyclical approach to time of archaic man, which in the last analysis nullifies history and with it any uniqueness of event, with the historical, linear approach of modern man that he sees as abandoning us in the end to the terror of history. Archaic humanity defended itself with all the weapons at its disposal against that very novelty and irreversibility that make up the essence of historical time. The archaic, or "primitive," human being like the mystic and the religious person in general, lives in a continual present in which he relives and repeats the gestures of another and, through this repetition, lives always in an atemporal present:

> What is of chief importance to us in these archaic systems is the abolition of concrete time, and hence their antihistorical intent. This refusal to preserve the memory of the past, even of the immediate past, seems to us to betoken ... archaic man's refusal to accept himself as a historical being, ... the will to devaluate time.[7]

In biblical Judaism, and hence in Judaism, Christianity, and Islam, there is affirmed for the first time "the idea that historical events have a value in themselves, insofar as they are determined by the will of God":

> Without finally renouncing the traditional concept of archetypes and repetitions, Israel attempts to "save" historical events by regarding them as active presences of Yahweh.... History no longer appears as a cycle that repeats itself *ad infinitum*, as the primitive peoples represented it.... Directly ordered by the will of Yahweh, history appears as a series of theophanies, negative or positive, each of which has its intrinsic value.[8]

Having set forth this contrast, Eliade advances numerous arguments against the historical view of time and in favor of the antihistorical, archaic view, which is also his own: the great majority of Jews and Christians have never accepted the historical view anyway; even the élite who accepted it looked forward to its abrogation in a Messianic age that places *illud tempore* at the end of time instead of the beginning; in the myth of the eternal return even history is taken up into archetypal time; even the three great history religions — the Iranian, Judaic, and Christian — "affirm that history will finally cease *in illo tempore*," thus reviving the ancient doctrine of the periodic regeneration of history; Marxism implies the overcoming of history in the "true" history that follows it, whereas various doctrines of historical immanentism, such as Nietzsche's and Heidegger's, have no relief to offer in the face of the terror of history. Eliade also contrasts the doctrines of progress and historical linearism of the modern world with the recrudescence of cyclical views of time in Spengler, Toynbee, and Sorokin and the longing for the return to the "golden age" in Joyce and T. S. Eliot.

Eliade, to be sure, sees Christianity as transcending, once for all, the old themes of eternal repetition and other archaic approaches to time by revealing the importance of the religious experience of faith, the value of the human personality, and the uniqueness of the fact of the Incarnation. Nonetheless, and by the same token, he sees Christianity as the religion of "fallen man"; for history and progress are both, in his view, a fall, "both implying the final abandonment of the paradise of archetypes and repetition." Lest we think this is simply a detached academic exposition, we must note Eliade's judgment on modern history. Though historical man might reproach archaic man with having sacrificed creativity through remaining imprisoned within the mythical horizon of archetypes and repetition, archaic man (speaking through Eliade) sees modern man as without defenses against the terror of history and, so far from being able to *make* history, as totally compelled and controlled by it:

> For history either makes itself ... or it tends to be made by an increasingly smaller number of men who not only prohibit the mass of their contemporaries from directly or indirectly intervening in the history they are making ..., but in addition have at their disposal means sufficient to force each individual to endure, for his own part, the consequences of this history, that is, to live immediately and continuously in dread of history. Modern man's boasted freedom to make history is illusory for nearly the whole of the human race.[9]

In contrast to this sorry fate of modern "historical" man, archaic man "can be proud of his mode of existence, which allows him to be free and to create. He is free to be no longer what he was, free to annul his own history through periodic abolition of time and collective regeneration." Christianity stands somewhere in between, because its new category of faith, which sees all things possible to man as well as God, emancipates man from any kind of natural "law" and constitutes the only new formula for man's collaboration with the creation since the traditional horizon of archetype and repetition was transcended.

> It is only by presupposing the existence of God that he conquers, on the one hand, freedom (which grants him autonomy in a universe governed by laws or, in other words, the "inauguration" of a mode of being that is new and unique in the universe and, on the other hand, the certainty that historical tragedies have a transhistorical meaning, even if that meaning is not always visible for humanity in its present condition. Any other situation of modern man leads, in the end to despair. It is a despair provoked not by his own human existentiality, but by his presence in a historical universe in which almost the whole of mankind lives prey to a continual terror (even if not always conscious of it).[10]

In the light of this situation, Christianity as the "religion of the 'fallen man,'" is, at least, the best of a very bad bargain!

Because of Eliade's eminence, because of his growing influence, because of the vast array of facts from the historical and archaic religions that he marshalls in support of his point of view, and because, on the face of it, his point of view seems the opposite of the approach that we are here taking toward history and myth, we must make some response to the thesis that he has so compellingly set forth.

One must distinguish, to begin with, between the validity of Eliade's thesis as the description of many archaic and not-so-archaic religious doctrines and as the overall point of view to which he wishes to elevate it. As he himself recognizes, what is in question here is a matter of interpretation, i.e., each set of facts may be interpreted from the standpoint of the other:

> The crucial difference between the man of the archaic civilizations and modern, historical man lies in the increasing value the latter gives to historical events, that is, to the "novelties" that, for traditional man, represented either meaningless conjunctures or infractions of norms (hence "faults," "sins," and so on) and that, as such, required to be expelled (abolished) periodically. The man who adopts the historical viewpoint would be justified in regarding the tra-

ditional conception of archetypes and repetition as an aberrant reidentification of history (that is, of "freedom" and "novelty") with nature (in which everything repeats itself). For, as modern man can observe, archetypes themselves constitute a "history" insofar as they are made up of gestures, acts, and decrees that, although supposed to have been manifested *in illo tempore*, were nevertheless manifested, that is, came to birth in time, "took place," like any other historical event.[11]

This recognition that archetypes are themselves born of historical events in no way invalidates those religions and myths that do rest upon an archetypal point of view in which all history is removed to sacred space and sacred time. But it does invalidate any general claim that *all* religious myth must be of this nature, and it supports what we have earlier observed concerning the historical and/or existential kernel even of universal myths.

The second response that we can make is that Eliade nowhere discusses faith as existential trust but sees it basically as a worldview that posits the existence of God and deduces from this the transhistorical meaning of history. Coupled with this is the fact that he regards historical and linear time only from the "apocalyptic" standpoint and not at all from the "prophetic":

> Since the days of Isaiah, a series of military defeats and political collapses had been anxiously awaited as an ineluctable syndrome of the Messianic *illud tempus* that was to regenerate the world.[12]

To appreciate the significance of this limitation in Eliade's understanding of the biblical approach to history, we must look, however briefly, at the two ideal types — prophetic and apocalyptic — that Martin Buber sets forth.

The Hebrew prophets sought God to "know" Him, to be in direct contact with Him, and not in order to hear future things. Even their predictions of the future were for the sake of the present, that the people might turn again to the way of God. Those who were pure prophets (as opposed to Ezekiel, Daniel, and Deutero-Isaiah, in whom various degrees of the apocalyptic were admixed) are distinguished from the apocalyptic ones, as from the seers and diviners of other religions, by the fact that they did not wish to peep into an already certain and immutable future but were concerned only with the full grasping of the present, both actual and potential. Their prophecy was altogether bound up with the situation of the historical hour and with God's direct speaking in it. They recognized the importance of man's decision in determining the future and therefore rejected any attempts to treat the future as if it were simply a fixed past which had not yet unfolded. Their attitude corresponds to the basic biblical view that man is set in real freedom in order that he may enter the dialogue with God and through this dialogue take part in the redemption of the world.

> The time the prophetic voice calls us to take part in is the time of the actual decision; to this the prophet summons his hearers ... In the world of the apocalyptic this present historical-biographical hour hardly ever exists, precisely because a decision by men constituting a factor in the historical-suprahistorical decision is not in question here. ... The apocalyptic writer ... does not really speak, he only writes.[13]

The time of the true prophet is not *illud tempore* but the experienced hour and its possibility. That of the apocalyptic writer is an inevitable future in which history is overcome. The prophetic approach to history "promises a consummation of creation," the apocalyptic "its abrogation and supersession by another world completely different in nature."

> The prophetic allows "the evil" to find the direction that leads toward God, and to enter into the good; the apocalyptic sees good and evil severed forever at the end of days, the good redeemed, the evil unredeemable for all eternity; the prophetic believes that the earth shall be hallowed, the apocalyptic despairs of an earth which it considers to be hopelessly doomed.[14]

Eliade's understanding of biblical Judaism and Christianity is essentially apocalyptic, not prophetic, which is not surprising considering that his own view of the "terror of history" is essentially

an apocalyptic one. Furthermore, though he recognizes a difference between the archaic and antihistorical religions and the historical ones, in the end he takes the antihistorical as the normative approach to all religions. He offers us as the objective conclusions of the historian of religion what is, in fact, the passionate choice of a "live forced option," in William James' phrase.
Nowhere is this clearer than in his discussion of "the East," by
which he apparently means Hinduism and early Buddhism:

> The East unanimously rejects the idea of the ontological ir-
> reducibility of the existent, even though it too sets out from
> a sort of "existentialism" (i.e., from acknowledging suffer-
> ing as the situation of any possible cosmic condition).
> Only, the East does not accept the destiny of the human
> being as final and irreducible. Oriental techniques attempt
> above all to annul or transcend the human condition. In
> this respect, it is justifiable to speak not only of freedom (in
> the positive sense) or deliverance (in the negative sense) but
> actually of creation; for what is involved is creating a new
> man and creating him on a suprahuman plane, a man-god,
> such as the imagination of historical man has never dreamed
> it possible to create.[15]

If we recognize this passionate statement for what it is — a
touchstone of reality representative of Eliade's own view — and
not as the necessary conclusion of the phenomenological study
of the history of religions, we can make it a part of our own dialogue of touchstones. Then, too, we can avoid the equal and opposite error of imposing a biblical view of history on non-history
religions. In the face of this, what general statements can we
make about myths? First, the one we have already made — that
some myths do, in fact, have a historical kernel and other, universal ones, an existential kernel, one that is repeated over and
over in the history of the human race. Second, that there are, indeed, myths that have come loose from both the historical and
the existential kernels that gave rise to them. This latter type of
myth, in its regular recurrence, gives rise to the perennial philosophies and theories of archetypes. But even here, "myth must
verify itself in man and not in myth." The archetypes too have a
human base and arise out of the loam of earthly, human exis-

tence. This in no way denies the archetypes, but it roots them in the lived concrete rather than in some Platonic universal or some mystical sphere floating above time and history. In this sense, we may echo Buber's words: "What is wrong is not the mythicization of reality which brings the inexpressible to speech, but the gnosticizing of myth which tears it out of the ground of history and biography in which it took root." What is inexpressible is that betweenness that lies at the heart of the life of dialogue. Myth is the pure form of the meeting. It points us back to the immediacy as no concepts could.

What we have said of legend and myth can also shed light on the relation between religion and literature. Some of the world's great literature, such as the Book of Genesis and the tragedies of Sophocles, is built upon myth. But even when it is not, literature in its very particularity is often far closer to religious reality than are the dogmas of theology or the abstractions of metaphysics. Literature retains much of the concreteness of persons and their interrelationships while at the same time enabling us to enter into a sufficiently close relationship with these persons so that they can speak to us as bearers of the human — as exemplifications of what it does and can mean to be a human being. It is for this reason that I claim in *To Deny Our Nothingness* that literature is the real homeland of the human image.

This does not mean a representational image, of course. Rather it means the characters of literature seen in the interactions through which they make manifest their basic life attitudes, their life-stances, and through which they acquire their own touchstones of reality — and become touchstones of reality for us, the readers.

This is exactly the opposite of that approach to religion and literature that seeks to extract religious symbols from the context of the literature and interpret them as if the literature were simply an allegory waiting for us to puzzle out its hidden meanings. If we approach literature looking for illustrations of a given philosophy or theology, we destroy the concreteness of our encounter with the literature and make it subservient to already fixed patterns of thought. To this attempt at finding meaning in symbols outside of the dynamic and dramatic event in which the symbol occurs I have given the name *symbolmongering*. When Queequeg's coffin-lifebuoy surfaces at the end of Melville's *Moby Dick*, it can be easily taken as a resurrection symbol, just as in Dostoevsky's novel *Crime and Punishment* there is a whole symbolism of Lazarus risen from the dead. Yet we dare not go from the symbol to the meaning of the novel unless that symbol has become dramatically real in the novel itself, as it has not in either book.

What is true of symbolmongering is also true of mythmongering. Both lie at the heart of the *mismeeting* between literature and religion. The collector's urge of modern man leads him to seek a universal myth in the myths of all peoples, whether it be that of the flood, of creation, or of the dragon and the dragon-slayer. These myths were the human being's first way of thinking — dramatic events rather than discursive reasoning. We try instead to derive a secondary meaning by identifying resemblances among myths. We extract a perennial myth and feel we are very close to the heart of reality when in fact we are freezing on the doorstep! Seldom if ever does a myth catch us up, as it did ancient man, so that for that moment all that is real and important is the heightened reality of the mythic event. The mythmonger asks us to accept a rich sense of everything having significant relation to everything else in place of any immediate insight into any particular event or reality. Both the symbolmonger and the mythmonger tend to see particular literary works as endlessly reproducing universal themes. In so doing they lose the very heart of religion, literature, and myth. They find the meaning of literature in the static symbol or concept and not in the concrete unique event and its dramatic, dynamic unfolding in time.

A very different approach to the relation between religion and literature is open to us if in the first instance we understand religion, as we have suggested, as a basic *attitude* or relationship arising in the encounter with the whole reality directly given to us in our existence. From this standpoint, many works of literature are as close to religious reality as any work of theology, for both may be products of some genuine religious encounter. This means taking seriously the full address of literature to the wholeness of the human. The most fruitful approach to the meeting of religion and literature is not to treat literature as if it were covert theology but to discover in our meeting with it that image of authentic human existence that is implicit in the very style of most great literature.

The image of the human, understood as a basic attitude toward reality, is a ground that is not identifiable in the first instance as literature, theology, religion, or philosophy, though having implications for all of them. Religion and literature do not meet in the once- or twice-remove of theology and literary criticism but in a matrix deeper and older than both of them. Originally literature was one of the basic expressions of numinous awe or wonder, as in the Vedic hymns and the Psalms. The Book of Job was not "the Bible as living literature"; it was living literature that was later taken into the Bible. We cannot recover those depths out of which the Book of Job came unless we can come with that openness and readiness to respond and even to be disturbed that very few bring to the reading of a text from the "Bible."

The meeting of religion and literature is not achieved by starting with the finished ideas of religion and then trying to find literature to illustrate them. We must, rather, dig deeper into both religion and literature so that we may recover and discover for ourselves that ground where they are one: those basic human attitudes that arise in our response to ultimate life-realities and to the daily life-situations that confront us. The notion that so many people have today — that meaning in literature is to be found most directly in the novel of ideas or the drama of ideas — is exactly backward. We reach the level of abstraction and timeless ideas only after hundreds of thousands of years of dealing with the more concrete in legend and in myth. Even drama began as a religious celebration; only much later did it acquire fixed roles and parts and become the detached drama of our stage. Religion and literature have a common matrix, and that matrix still informs their meeting, when it takes place. Literature, indeed, is often far closer to original religious reality than any of its later objectifications in creed, doctrine, theology, and metaphysics.

All this is so, of course, only if the reader enters into a dialogue with literature in real openness, risking, venturing, and responding. This openness to meaning at all levels implies an openness to being changed by our encounter with literature. This openness is made possible through that existential and interhuman trust that makes us willing to give ourselves imaginatively into the hands of the poet or author. This interhuman trust, this readiness to be open and respond without any prior commitment to assent, accounts for the possibility of an image of the human or a touchstone of reality coming alive for us in our meeting with literature, as Coleridge's "willing suspension of disbelief" could never do. Combined with obedient listening and faithful response to the voice of the other that addresses us in novel, poem, or play, this personal involvement enables us to take literature out of the brackets of the purely aesthetic or the merely didactic. Only then can our own image of the human, our own touchstone of reality enter into dialogue with the image of the human or touchstone of reality underlying the work that confronts us. If religion means bringing the whole of one's existence into dialogue with the "nameless Meeter," then literature as genuine personal dialogue must be an integral part of religious reality as we know it. Religion and literature, then, would not be thought of as different modes or languages, however much theology and literary criticism may be properly spoken of in that way, but as differing degrees of fullness of a single dialogical reality. If this means in one sense subsuming our dialogue with literature under our meeting with ultimate reality, it means in a still deeper sense that our meeting with ultimate reality takes place only within the very structures and events of our concrete daily existence, no unimportant part of which is our dialogue with literature.[16]

What is said here also applies to that popular form of contemporary literature that we call biography. Much contemporary biography is really fiction, a deliberately novelized version of a life to lend connections and meanings where none may be. But even where the biographer has greater faithfulness to his subject than to the mass audience for which he writes, there is, of course, an element of selection, of art, and even of legend and mythicization that enters in. We do not need to ask that a biography be true to the "facts," for life itself is something more than a collection of facts. Yet we may fairly ask for an honest faithfulness that tries to bring before us a unique human reality that otherwise we might not be able to enter into dialogue with.

A letter of gratitude that Martin Buber wrote in 1953 for an essay on the life of his old friend Oskar Loerke expresses this relation between biography, dialogue, and the human image in a classic manner. "Your essay not only enriched Loerke's image in my memory," wrote Buber, "but made it truly an image for the first time. For the image of a dear departed is not, in fact, a fixed one but a shape that changes through real time." This observation takes on particular poignancy in light of the fact that Loerke is one of the three friends who Buber believed died of guilt for their participation in the cultural activities of Nazi Germany!

My own conviction of the interrelation of biography, dialogue, and the image of the human led me to coin the term *dialography* as a description of my three-volume book *Martin Buber's Life and Work.* With this term I sought to point out the central purpose of that work — the attempt to show Buber's thought and *oeuvre* as his active personal response to the events and meetings of his life. In the course of a dozen years of work on "Encounter on the Narrow Ridge," I became convinced of the fundamental falsification that is often introduced by the evolutionary or developmental approach to biography. This struck me particularly vividly when I read Dag Hammarskjøld's *Markings* in preparation for my chapter on Buber and Hammarskjøld. To understand the meeting and the continuing dialogue between these two great men, I would need to understand what most biographers necessarily leave out of account: the uniqueness of each person taken in himself *and* the unique, present meeting between them that can never be grasped as merely a sum of their two uniquenesses. In any case, I could never regard Hammarskjøld as merely a part of Buber's environment or as merely an event within the flow of Buber's personal becoming. Biography leads us to see events as clustered about a life — as if the event were contained in the life rather than, as is actually the case, the *life* in the events. To see the event — a meeting with other persons and situations — as merely part of a life process or development is necessarily to see it one-sidedly. To see the life in the event, in contrast, is to begin to glimpse the profound two-sidedness of every event.

The title that Buber placed above the Hasidic tale in which Rabbi Leib comes to see the Maggid of Mezritch to watch him lace and unlace his felt shoes, "Not to Say Torah but to Be Torah," is not, as it might seem, a contrast between what a person is and what a person says. Rather, it is the basic way in which we speak to one another — through what we are. The whole person, who has brought his or her inner contradictions into some meaningful personal direction, communicates "Torah" — instruction and guidance on the way — even by his or her most casual and unintentional acts. All a person's gestures, utterances, and actions bear the stamp of the unique person that he or she is. This person will also teach in words, but what he or she *is* is the guarantor of what he or she *says*. In another tale the same Rabbi Leib contrasts apparent speaking, mere words, and real speaking, with or without words: "What does it amount to — that they expound the Torah! A man should see to it that all his actions are a Torah and that he himself becomes so entirely a Torah that one can learn from his habits and his motions and his motionless clinging to God." If this is so, not only can a unique, concrete event underlie a legend, myth, or tale, but the telling of a tale may itself be an event, as when the lame disciple was healed while showing how the Baal Shem danced! The Maggid of Mezritch once said to his disciples:

I shall teach you the best way to say Torah. You must cease to be aware of yourselves. You must be nothing but an ear which hears what the universe of the word is constantly saying within you. The moment you start hearing what you yourself are saying, you must stop.[17]

Part three

Solitude and Community

6

Inwardness and the Life of Dialogue

If a person were in such a rapturous state as St. Paul once entered, and he knew of a sick man who wanted a cup of soup, it would be far better to withdraw from the rapture for love's sake and serve him who is in need.

A long time ago in China there were two friends, one who played the harp skillfully and one who listened skillfully.

When the one played or sang about a mountain, the other would say: "I can see the mountain before us."

When the one played about water, the listener would exclaim: "Here is the running stream!"

But the listener fell sick and died. The first friend cut the strings of his harp and never played again.

When a man is singing and cannot lift his voice, and another comes and sings with him, another who can lift his voice, then the first will be able to lift his voice too. That is the secret of the bond between spirit and spirit.[1]

THE HINDU SEARCH for superconsciousness and for enlightenment raises the question of whether the essence of the true person is to be found in consciousness or in the whole person. Is it found by leaving the world that is given to us — the social world, the world of nature, the world of the senses? Or is it found by remaining in relation to the life of the senses and to other people? Is the goal of man enlightenment and individual spiritual salvation or is it a way of life that does not attain individual perfection yet affirms and redeems the human world? When inwardness and inner spiritual development are seen as the goal of life, external actions tend to become relativized. As a result, the problem of ethics is never a problem of "What ought I do in this situation?" but of "What is the spiritual stage I have reached and what is the right way for me to act in terms of this spiritual stage?"

Many religions confront us with the question of whether the highest and most authentic existence is not that in which not only lust but also the total post-Freudian attitude toward sex as a wholesome and natural thing must be overcome in favor of the use of this energy for spiritual enlightenment. Gandhi suggests that the highest stage is the stage of chastity. But one finds the same in Saint Paul who says, "I wish you could be chaste, even as I, but if you cannot contain, it is better to marry than to burn." All over the world, in fact, there are mystics who suggest that the highest way is the way that overcomes the "vulgar sexual act," and directs its energy toward God. They believe that the goal of spiritual perfection demands all of your energies — not just on the level they now are, but transformed and elevated through concentration and devotion — to become the basis of a whole new state of spiritual being. One cannot leave aside any part of one to do this.

On the other hand, there is here an implied dualism not only between spirit and flesh, but also between individual consciousness and the social world, which is considered, if not an evil world, at least a lesser world. The two of these factors work together to induce us to concentrate attention on the inner, on inward spiritual perfection, the realization of our spiritual essence. This constitutes a great issue in the history of religions, one that excludes the possibility of any common "essence" that could be extracted from all religions. Does one hold that the true goal of spiritual existence is this sort of inner perfection in which one relates to the world either as a hindrance or as a stepping-stone to this perfection? Or does one believe that what is asked of one is a completion of the world that will forever leave oneself imperfect? Hasidism, the popular communal Jewish mysticism of the eighteenth to twentieth centuries, holds that there is a third alternative to giving oneself over to the phantasmagoric play of the satisfaction of the senses and of lust, on the one hand, or leaving that behind and trying to move altogether into an individual sphere of chastity, on the other — namely, serving God with the "evil" urge.

The great modern philosopher Alfred North Whitehead defined religion as what man does with his solitariness. My teacher, Joachim Wach, in his book *Sociology of Religion*, says that, world-over, religion is a phenomenon of groups, whether it be the original disciples clustered around the master, the brotherhood, the sect, the denomination, the church, or the *Imam* the wider Islamic brotherhood. The history of most religions confirms this. Early Buddhism was intensely concerned with the career of the Arhat, the individual seeking release from an existence of suffering through attaining Nirvana. Yet, even so, early Buddhism was centrally concerned with the *Sangha*, the brotherhood of monks, and each individual monk was obliged not only to seek for his own salvation but to follow the Buddha in going out to "turn the wheel of the doctrine."

Even the early Christian anchorites who lived in the desert, often a great many miles from anyone else, had a real sense of brotherhood and an intense concern with one another.

This does not get us to the heart of the issue, however. Most of those today who are concerned with attaining one or another type of "altered consciousness" are *not* concerned with getting away from the company of other human beings entirely. In his famous Naylor Sonnets, the well-known economist Kenneth Boulding, who was a mystic before it became a contemporary fad to be one, asks:

> Can I have fellowship with them
> Who fed on locusts
> And on husks of swine,
> Slept without tent,
> Went naked as a sign,
> And made the unforgiving
> Earth their bed,

When I with gentle raiment
Have been clothed,
And have sat down to dine
And slept comforted?[2]

Boulding concludes that he *can* join the Christian anchorites only in the "fellowship in the deserts of the mind." Since Boulding wrote those sonnets, "inner space," as we like to call it, has become a notoriously *group* phenomenon, whether in the communes and drug experiments of the 1960s, the flowering of growth groups and the Human Potential Movement, or the various neo-Oriental cults that have arisen, from Meher Baba and Subudh to Hare Krishna and Rajneesh.

The issue must be grasped, rather, in terms of ultimate touchstones of reality. There is nothing about turning inward that altogether or always excludes community, and there is nothing about community that excludes turning inward. Yet there *is* the question of whether our inwardness means, at some level, a turning away from the life of the senses and from contact with our fellow human beings and whether community means the sacrifice of precisely that detachment that would enable us to turn inward and grow in spiritual enlightenment.

As soon as one brings in the phrase *life of dialogue* (which I've taken from the subtitle of my early book on Martin Buber's thought), the issue before us is significantly changed. The traditional contrasts between individual and society are always a distortion of concrete reality because no individual lives without being part of society in some sense and cannot, therefore, meaningfully be set in contrast to it. Even setting individualism against collectivism is a distortion, not because these two emphases do not exist but because, formulated that way, it appears that they represent two basic human realities, excluding any others. The life of dialogue, in contrast, recognizes that, more concrete than these abstractions, the basic human category is person with person, self with self. This does not mean simply the I-Thou relationship; for we exist in other modes as well. It means that man is a *zoon politikon*, a "political animal," as Aristotle put it, that the self is social. But this social self need not imply, as

George Herbert Mead thought, that the self is merely an eddy in the social current, any more than it means that society is merely an aggregate of individual selves. Individualism and collectivism arise as emphases precisely because they are *secondary*, not primary, human realities. The primary human reality is the self in dialogue, in family, in community. The individual and society are both abstractions from this reality.

The problem is further complicated by our tendency to think in terms of *inner* versus *outer*. We speak of some people as *inner directed* and others as *outer directed*, of some as *introverts*, literally those who turn inward, and others as *extroverts*, literally those who turn outward. My old friend Rollo May was decisively influenced both by the theologian Søren Kierkegaard, with his emphasis on the single, authentic individual person, and by the American psychiatrist Harry Stack Sullivan, with his emphasis on the *interpersonal*. Part of the standing dialogue between Rollo May and myself over the last 20 years has been his tendency to see Buber's thought as basically in line with Sullivan, the turning outward to the social, and my contention that it represents a really third position between Kierkegaard and Sullivan. In the same way, in my dialogue with some of my close friends who are Jungians, I have occasionally been shocked to discover both Buber and myself labeled as extroverts, as if the life of dialogue meant turning to the other at the expense of one's own inwardness.

The issue here is not whether inwardness may be dispensed with — I do not think that it can — but whether one aims at it as one's ultimate goal. Is our life in the world the steppingstone to mystical contemplation or do we grow in inwardness precisely so that we can go out again and again to meet what comes to meet us? The Jungians contend that individuation is necessary not only for the realization of the self but also for any meaningful relation with others. Insofar as our relations are distorted by our *shadows* — our introjections and projections — this is undoubtedly the case. "Dialogue between individuals is merely a sketch," says Buber in his essay, "Dialogue." Only dialogue between real persons is dialogue in the full sense of the term. But one does not become a real person by turning away from others and focusing on one's own individuation, with the hope of later turning more effectively to others: "By what could a man from being an individual so really become a person," writes Buber, "as by the strict and sweet experience of dialogue which teaches him the boundless contents of the boundary?"

The boundary is real. We do not simply merge with others in some symbiotic oneness. The ever-renewed distancing is as essential to the life of dialogue as the ever-renewed relating. "Dialogue does not mean that call for universal unreserve that is heard in twilight ages," Buber writes in "Dialogue." "He who shares his substance with every passerby has no substance to lose." In "The Question to the Single One," his *Auseinandersetzung* with Kierkegaard, Buber goes even further and says that if we do not want to see our relation to others dissipate into the infinite, we must cultivate an inner-worldly monastic solitude with all the strictness of the monastery. This going inward to solitude and out to meet others from that solitude is "the systole and diastole" of the soul.

If religion *were* what one does with one's solitariness alone, as Whitehead says, then an all-important part of our existence would be cut off from religion, and religion would necessarily be an expression of the exception or fragmentation of life rather than its wholeness. Yet much that we have identified with religion down through the ages — prayer, mystic ecstasy, contemplation, *samadhi*, nirvana — *seems* to be just what Whitehead claimed. But it seems to be this way because the modern mystic, in contrast to the mystics of the ages, tends to isolate the mystical experience from its full communal, social, and traditional context and just thereby misses its essence. In searching for *the* mystic experience, we may lose the concrete uniqueness and the social significance of the mystical life. The ancient Hindu took the social order, with its castes and caste duties, for granted; it was as much a part of the *dharma* as the individual himself. The modern neo-Hindu leaves out that order in favor of the individual aspect of the experience alone.

In the Upanishads, the relation of the self to other selves is either replaced by or reduced to self-relationship — the relation of the self to itself. The *self* that is left, as a result, is stripped of all essential characteristics of the ordinary self that we know in our day-by-day relationships, save consciousness. It no longer has personality, character, name, social relations, body, mind, individuality. It does not even have uniqueness, for the value and reality of the self lie in the Universal Self within and not in any unique personal stance in relation to the world. From this concern with essence, it follows that the true Self is independent of the body in which it dwells, and therefore the true Self is immortal. We are aware of the self as detached from what we habitually associate with it — sense impressions, name, form, social relations. Somehow each of us has a sense of transcending all these things, no matter how aware we may be at the same time of the self as constituted within all of these things. Finally, according to mystics the world over, we find, by going within, an intensified consciousness that not only is ineffable and all-absorbing, including every other sensation, reflection, and concern, but also is a self-evident and self-guaranteeing reality of existence, compared to which our waking consciousness seems unreal. The dreamer dreams that the dream is real, but when waking knows that it is only a dream compared to the waking consciousness. Similarly, when we attain this higher consciousness, our waking world seems to us, in comparison, a dream. Thus the world is unreal *only* in comparison with this higher reality.

The familiar metaphor of life as a dream is illuminating if we examine it in depth. The Hindu concept of existence as *maya* is often translated as "illusion." But we are in no position to understand this concept if we imagine that somehow the world of the senses, *nama-rupa*, name and form, good and evil, are all relative, while we remain in our individual selves absolute. The fact is that our consciousness of self is just as relative as the world. What is more, we cannot even grasp this notion of relativity except in relation to some higher consciousness to which we are awakened. Therefore, enlightenment is always compared in one form or another to an awakening from a dream: "From the unreal lead us to the real, from darkness to light, from death to immortality." Our dreams are not unreal but, relative to our waking lives, they are, or seem to be, less real. Similarly, our waking lives are not unreal; yet relative to *samadhi*, a higher mystical consciousness that we can attain, they may seem relatively unreal.

None of this implies that for the ancient Hindu the social is any less real than the individual; quite the contrary. Yet the perspective that this metaphor of the dream lends us may, nonetheless, be misleading. It takes for granted consciousness, whether it be the individual consciousness as for Descartes ("I think, therefore I am") or the fuller consciousness of Brahman is Atman and Thou Art That, as *the* touchstone of reality. What we are comparing is the relative reality of levels of consciousness. But the full existence of the person in community is not a matter of consciousness alone. If we do not accept the idealist philosopher's identification of thought and reality, we shall have to acknowledge that in meeting the "things of this world" and in meeting other persons we are not just expanding our own consciousness. We are, instead, having contact with a reality that transcends our consciousness — not just our Cartesian consciousness of individuality but consciousness itself.

This notion of transcending consciousness was so unthinkable to Edmund Husserl, the idealist founder of the philosophy of phenomenology, that he saw the unfolding of the universe as one vast *egology*, our understanding of other selves as by analogy with our own selves, and selves themselves as only meeting within the field of consciousness that he called the *transcendent ego*. Jean-Paul Sartre, rightly, wanted to get beyond this in his existential phenomenology. Yet he managed to get no further than seeing the consciousness placed in front of him as a freedom that robbed him of his own freedom, a look that turned him into an object, or a lover who wanted to possess him as a person, to be sure, but only as a person subjected to his domination.

If persons meet, this is not a meeting of minds but of whole existences, and just in that meeting, as in our meeting with any concrete existent (from the clothes hanging on the hammock outside my window to the Siamese cat making its way around my swimming pool), we come to the limits of our own consciousness. The contact with others through which our touchstones of reality come into existence can give us no knowledge of those others as they are minus our relation to them. Yet it is, for all that, a contact with real otherness that communicates the limit-edness of the very consciousness that in our world views and mystic ecstasies seems to us unlimited. In our human life togeth-er we build a common reality that comes from just this meeting with otherness, this transcendence of consciousness. Hence this reality can never properly be grasped from the analogy of the greater reality of the dreamer than the dream, focusing as it does on consciousness alone and leaving out the limits of conscious-ness that are vouchsafed us in our contacts with other existing beings.

The significance of this contrast between touchstones of reality will elude us, however, if we still think in terms of the contrast inner and outer. Inner versus outer splits reality into two opposing parts and practically forces us to lay emphasis upon one as opposed to the other as the more basic reality. Thus, I have pointed out (in *To Deny Our Nothingness*) that both Bergson and Jung, the "Modern Vitalist" and the "Modern Gnostic," exalt the inner as the higher reality and tend to deprecate the outer as merely the social or, in Jung's terms, the *persona*, the mask, or social role, that we assume in the social world. But the celebrated American psychologist, B. F. Skinner, I have referred to as a "sawed-off dualist" (*The Hidden Human Image*) because *he* makes the outer the real and contemptuously dismisses the inner as a "homunculus" that we have made up to lend freedom and dignity to abstractions that have no reality in themselves! It is significant that Skinner also relegates the I-Thou relationship to the inner, even as some Jungians relegate it to the outer, since given this false either/or, there is no room for the re-ality of the *between*.

Inner and outer, however, are *not* primordial human reality but secondary elaborations and constructions arising from a hu-man wholeness that precedes them both. Unless we understand this and understand the possibility of direct contact between whole human beings, we cannot understand the sphere of the be-tween and its claim to be a touchstone of reality. The inner is psychic in the sense that we do not perceive anything with our senses, the outer physical in the sense that we do. And these di-visions are useful for a certain ordering of our lives, such as the distinction between what we see, what we dream, what we envision, and what we hallucinate! It is no accident that Descartes, in establishing modern philosophy, left it with a deep-seated dualism between mind and body — "unextended thinking thing" and "extended non-thinking thing." Yet if we think about human existence in its wholeness, we realize that a true event in our lives is neither inner nor outer but takes up and claims the whole of us. The meeting between persons, what is more, is hardly a mere going outward; for in its depth such meeting includes our penetrating to the very heart of the other by "imagining the real." Only from such a meeting, in fact, can we know that there is not just *one* inner — myself — and *one* outer — others. Sartre to the contrary notwithstanding, the other's inwardness does not mean I must be merely outer for him — a part of the environment to be ingested and used — any more than he need be merely outer for me. Only if we can get beyond this deep-seated prejudice of inner and outer can we understand the sense in which our existential meetings — whether with persons, animals, plants, or rocks — are, in their betweenness, meetings with the Ultimate. Just as every electron has a finite center and an infinite circumference, so we each have our own ground yet meet each other from that ground. Our existences interpenetrate. Inner versus outer is thus not only a distortion of the primordial human wholeness of the person, but also a distortion of the reality of our existence as person *with* person.

We are now in a position to look at the claim that in our meeting with the everyday, we can, and sometimes do, meet the Ultimate, that the events of our lives are not only contacts with otherness but encounters that leave us with *touchstones of reality*. This claim is only comprehensible in terms of the sphere of the *between*; for it is not a claim that any particular person or thing we meet is itself the Ultimate. This would, indeed, be idolatry, and it is to rescue us from such vulgar anthropomorphism that many philosophies and religions have identified the "really real" with what is met outside of time and space and the world of the senses. Biblical Judaism, like Islam and some parts of Hinduism and Christianity, is an exception to this. The God to which it points is an imageless God, the Creator of time and space who transcends the world that he creates. Yet that does not mean that we cannot meet God in the world; for God is immanent — not in the sense of being some universal essence inside of particulars but in the sense that each thing that we meet can be a *Malach*, an angel or messenger that speaks to us of God, a burning bush that tells us that the ground on which we stand — the ground of the everyday — is the ground of hallowing and that we can know this if we but put the shoes off our feet, i.e., put off the habitual that hides from us the fact that each moment is "full of enormous lights and mysteries." Our touchstones of reality are not the miracles of the past but the revelation of the present, and even the touchstones we have inherited from the past are important to us only because "Not our fathers but we the living stand on Mount Sinai to receive the Torah." It is us, not our fathers, whom the Lord leads each day out of slavery to the land that he will show us.

This relation between past and present touchstones is beautifully captured by Zusya, one of my favorite Hasidic rabbis, in "Get Thee Out of Thy Country":

> God said to Abraham: "Get thee out of thy country, and from thy kindred, and from thy father's house, unto the land that I will show thee." God says to man: "First, get you out of your country, that means the dimness you have inflicted on yourself. Then out of your birth-place, that means, out of the dimness your mother inflicted on you. After that, out of the house of your father, that means, out of the dimness your father inflicted on you. Only then will you be able to go to the land that I will show you."[3]

Unlike the psychoanalysts, Zusya does not teach us to begin by removing the projections inflicted on us by our father and mother and only then lead us to a "reality testing" of the present. Rather we must begin where we are in the present, by casting off the dimness that we have inflicted on ourselves, and only then will we be able to disburden ourselves of the dimness inflicted on us by our father and our mother!

This relationship of past and present touchstones lies at the heart of the only continuity that can be found in the life of dialogue — the renewed meeting with the Thou so that the past relationship is renewed and given new meaning in the unique relationship of the present. In this dialogical understanding lies the most important meeting point of the two central metaphors that I have developed: that of the human image and touchstones of reality. We can discover the image of the human in the concrete precisely because we have no access to the human via any abstract universal but only by our dialogue with past images of the human that become present to us and enter into our meeting with the present. The famous poem of the nineteenth-century English Catholic poet Francis Thompson, "The Kingdom of Heaven is Within Us" or "In No Strange Land," combines Jacob's touchstone of reality, his vision of the ladder reaching from earth to heaven, and that of Jesus' disciples, their vision of the master walking on the Sea of Galilee, with the images of the human that Jacob and Jesus had bequeathed him and sees them both as present reality in the London of his day. The "God-forsaken" wilderness into which Jacob fled from the wrath of his brother Esau, whose birthright he had stolen by trickery, is now the equally "God-forsaken" London in whose streets Thompson died as an alcoholic, and the river on which Christ walked is now the Thames! But only because "the many-splendoured thing" is found not in the far reaches of the stars but right here in the commonplace and fallen world — London's "chartered streets" beside "the chartered Thames" that a century earlier William Blake had written of.

> O world invisible we view Thee,
> O world intangible we touch Thee,
> O world unknowable we know Thee,
> Inapprehensible we clutch Thee.
>
> Does the fish soar to find the ocean,
> The eagle plunge to find the air
> That we ask of the stars in motion
> If they have rumor of Thee there?
>
> Not where the wheeling systems darken
> And our benumbed conceiving soars,
> The drift of pinions, would we hearken,
> Beats at our own clay-shuttered doors.

[Even in his servants he puts no trust,
and his angels he charges with error;
how much more those who dwell in houses of clay....

Job 4:18-19, RSV]

The angels keep their ancient places,
Turn but a stone and start a wing.
'Tis ye, 'tis your estranged faces
That miss the many-splendoured thing.

But when so sad thou canst not sadder,
Cry, and on thy so sore loss
Shall shine the traffic of Jacob's ladder
Pitched betwixt Heaven and Charing Cross.

Yea in the night my soul, my daughter,
Cry, clinging Heaven by the hems,
And lo Christ walking on the water
Not of Genessareth but Thames!

We meet the "nameless Meeter" in the overwhelming and uncanny, Rudolf Otto's "Mysterium Tremendum" that fascinates
and terrifies us. But we can also meet it in beauty and warmth
and in the call and demand of the everyday. The wonder of existence is not found merely in its galaxies and black holes but in
the grain of sand and the blade of grass, the kittens that play
with one another, the breeze caressing the stream. No one has
understood this with greater clarity or expressed it with greater
conciseness and beauty than Lao-tzu in the *Tao Te Ching, The
Way of Life*:

> Existence is beyond the power of words
> To define:
> Terms may be used
> But are none of them absolute.

In the Hindu Vedanta it is only Brahman, the One without Second; in the metaphysics of Plato and Aristotle it is only the Good
or the Unmoved Mover that cannot be defined. The very nature
of finite existence to these latter implies that it can be delimited
into name and form, same and other, category and class. For

Zen Buddhism and Taoism, in contrast, it is existence itself that is illimitable and ineffable. In Taoism both the core and the surface are essentially the same.

> If name be needed, wonder names them both:
> From wonder into wonder
> Existence opens.

Plato said that wonder is the beginning of philosophy, but the philosopher, as Martin Buber has said, neutralizes his wonder in doubt. From Descartes to the present even the beginning of philosophy is not wonder, but doubt. Only here and there — in William Blake's aphorisms, "How do you know but that every bird that wings its way through the air is a whole world of delight closed to your senses five?", in Francis Thompson's "many-splendoured thing"; in the philosophy of Abraham Joshua Heschel, who sees each thing as pointing beyond itself and grounds all knowledge, art, and religion on "the awareness of the ineffable" — is any comparable insight found in the Western world. The one name that does not falsify existence, dividing it up and closing it off, is wonder: "From wonder into wonder existence opens." Taoism, like Zen Buddhism and Hasidism, is an existential mysticism, a mysticism of the particular, in which the concrete, precisely in its concreteness, reveals vista upon vista to the eye of the person who meets it in openness. The senses are not "bad witnesses," as Gerald Heard once wrote, misquoting Heraclitus, but, as Heraclitus himself said, are only "bad witnesses to those who have barbarian souls"!

The metaphysician and Gnostic, from Plato to the present, discriminates between the real world and mere appearance or phenomena, setting the goal of the true philosopher as ascending beyond the world of the senses to a face-to-face confrontation with absolute reality. Lao-tzu, in contrast, is content to allow the ultimate reality to speak in the only way in which it can speak to us — through its images. This ultimate reality for him is not some unmovable, self-sufficient absolute but the core, the womb of life, that constantly gives birth to the concrete realities that, changing and evanescent though they be, are as real as the Tao which flows through them. Although "the source appears dark emptiness," actually it

> Brims with a quick force
> Farthest away
> And yet nearest at hand
> From oldest time unto this day,
> Charging its images with origin:
> What more need I know of the origin
> Than this?

We do not have to look beyond seeing for "the unseen" or beyond hearing for "the unheard." The true oneness "forever sends forth a succession of living things as mysterious / As the unbegotten existence to which they return." Men have called these living things "empty phenomena / Meaningless images, / In a mirage / With no face to meet, / No back to follow." But that is because they insist on setting up a dualism between "mere appearance" and some entirely hidden, unmanifested Reality. The true meaning of *phenomenon,* as Martin Heidegger has pointed out in our day, is precisely that it shows forth and manifests Being, and Being is not a static absolute but the very ground of existence in time. This cannot be known through philosophical reflection alone, however, but only through the way of life that allows the Tao to flow through us and between us and all beings, rounding the way of earth and of heaven. "One who is anciently aware of existence / Is master of every moment." There is no split for us between the eternal and the present, the origin and the immediate. Our mastery is our openness in depth to what each moment tells us of origin. Flowing with life, we "feel no break since time beyond time / In the way life flows."

To this even Heidegger does not attain. For him "man" is the "shepherd of Being," the existent being through whom Being can attain its "unconcealment," and the Logos of Heraclitus is the silent word of Being that the authentic person lets sound forth. But this is to transpose the mystic absolute into the language of time without the concreteness of the interaction between person and person, person and "thing." That is why in *The Hidden Human Image,* I set the Hasidic teaching that we are called upon "to be *humanly* holy, in the measure and manner of man" in contrast to Heidegger's later teaching of an evocation of a new procession of images of the holy through man, the existing Being through whom Being is led into unconcealment. Heidegger's metaphysical ontology of Being has as its consequence a reduction of the concrete image of the human and of the relationship and "word" between one human being and another to a secondary, "ontic" position, that is, to a mere phenomenological manifestation of Being in existence, which is not fully real in itself.

If the Hebrew Bible asks "What is man?" who is dwarfed by the heavens yet has dominion over the creatures (Psalm 8), it also points to the nonanthropomorphic reality of creation that exceeds human scope and comprehension and to the solicitude, not of man but of God "who causes it to rain on a land where no man is, to satisfy the desolate and waste land" (Job). "Being-there," wrote Heidegger in *The Introduction to Metaphysics* (1936), "signifies care of the ecstatically manifest being of the essence as such, not only of human being. . . . Being-there is *itself* by virtue of its essential relation to being in general." Although Heidegger subordinates our human existence to that metaphysical-mystical Being that he regards as ultimate, he sees the human being as having the very special task that nothing else in existence has, of allowing, helping, and actualizing the unfolding and historical manifestation of this Being. This is something that the existent cannot do of itself. So, if Heidegger emphatically rejects Sartre's definition of existentialism as "a humanism," he nonetheless arrogates for the human a place even more important than that given it by traditional biblical religion. The essence of being human, to Heidegger, is precisely the need of Being for a place of disclosure. The being-there of historical man is the breach through which the being embodied in the essence can open. As a result, "the question of how it stands with being proves to be the question of how it stands with our being-there in history, the question of whether we *stand* in history or merely stagger." Not expecting the modern "pastry cooks" of philosophy, "the tired latecomers with their supercilious wit," to understand this question, Heidegger answered it himself: "From a metaphysical point of view, we *are staggering*. We . . . no longer know how it stands with being," and we do not know that we no longer know.

Heidegger to the contrary, it is not Being but man that is in need of unconcealment, for "the bowels of existence," in Nietzsche's words, "only speak to man as man." Man is not "the shepherd of Being" but the bearer of the truly human in the midst of the uniquely personal. "When I get to heaven," said Rabbi Zusya shortly before his death, "they will not ask me, 'Why were you not Moses?' but 'Why were you not Zusya?'" At the same time, biblical man, Hasidic man, and the "sound man" of Lao-tzu understand and embody the action of the whole being in its flowing interaction with everything it meets. In this flowing interaction the old paradox reemerges — that we find authentic existence, realize our true selves, manifest our true uniqueness not through aiming directly at it but through opening ourselves to and going out to meet what is not ourselves. Only thus do we immerse our selves in the stream of the Tao that is within, between, and beyond all creatures.

> A sound man by not advancing himself
> Stays the further ahead of himself
> By not confining himself to himself
> Sustains himself outside himself:
> By never being an end in himself
> He endlessly becomes himself.

We are so used to thinking of the spiritual life as a goal that we set out directly to attain mystic self-realization, enlightenment, even saintliness. Instead of allowing our becoming to take place naturally and spontaneously as a byproduct of the way we meet life, we make ourselves an end in ourselves and thus distort and pervert the very means that we use.

For Lao-tzu, remaining at the center of one's being does not mean turning away from one's fellows, but responding to them from that very core. "A sound man's heart is not shut within itself / But is open to other people's hearts."[4] It also means recognizing that other people do not possess fixed character — good or evil, honest or dishonest — but that the way in which I approach them, the way in which I allow the Tao to flow between myself and them frees them to possibilities of goodness, trust,

and openness, just as my mistrust and categorizing make it difficult for them to break out of habitual modes of dishonesty and
mistrust.

> I find good people good,
> And I find bad people good
> If I am good enough;
> I trust men of their word,
> And I trust liars
> If I am true enough;
> I feel the heart-beats of others
> Above my own
> If I am enough of a father,
> Enough of a son.

"Bad people" and liars are not bad and dishonest the way a table
is a table or a chair a chair. Approached with openness and
trust, they may be able to respond in kind. Approached with
hatred and distrust, they will be confirmed in the mold in which
their earlier interactions have already fixed them.

What can we conclude from all this about the relation of the
self to religious experience? The self in its integrity, its
uniqueness, and its individuality is indispensable to religious
experience, not, however, as the subject and center of that
experience but as the sharer and participant in a religious reality
that transcends it. There are depths within the self that largely
lie unexplored, and it is for this reason that an emphasis upon
the need of centering and inwardness, or what the Quakers call
"the inward light," is not amiss. Yet it is not simply by voyaging
inward — to the archetypal depths that unfold to us when we
attain individuation or even to the nondualistic, nonindividual
Self of the Upanishads — that the self becomes a sharer in
religious reality. For to do this leads to that other paradox that
is the counterpart of Lao-tzu's "By never being an end in
himself, he endlessly becomes himself," namely, that in transcending and denying the self and going inward one ends up in
absolutely affirming the Self. At this point the dangers of [self-]
"inflation" against which Jung warned are real indeed. Nor is the

ground that the self has thereby attained as shoreless and infinite as it first appears. Without the life of dialogue, without the genuine meeting with otherness that cannot be removed into the self (or even the Self), some part of the wholeness of human existence, and with it the address to us of the divine in the particular, will deny itself to us.

The corollary of this is not simply an emphasis upon religious community as opposed to solitude. Religious community, as we have seen, may itself block the renewal of our unique touchstones, and this is especially so when one ceases to hold the tension of being simultaneously a "Single One" and a responsible member of one's family, group, or community. We do not seek simple unity in which we all merge into one, but neither do we seek the loose structure of a community of affinity, or likemindedness, in which we "confirm" one another as sharing one same world view while essentially having little to do with one another aside from church socials and games or gatherings at the Jewish community center.

Perhaps if we were to use the word *communion* in its original, nontechnical, nonspecifically religious sense, we might indicate better what we are pointing toward; for communion suggests fellowship without unity. My own phrase *the community of otherness* may take on meaning in this respect when we come to discuss modern pluralism and the dialogue of touchstones. The prophets of the Hebrew Bible certainly knew the difference between that loose association we commonly call *community* and the genuine community of communion, the community of otherness. They called people to turn their existences away from false community and back to God in order to make real the Covenant in true community. "God demands not 'religion' but community," says Buber, paraphrasing Jeremiah.

At first glance, it may seem impossible to link the emphasis on wonder with which we started and the prophetic demand for moral and social change. Yet that is exactly what Abraham Joshua Heschel does in his philosophy of religion, spanning as it does the "awareness of the ineffable" and the prophet's indignation at our lack of concern for one another. The person who becomes immersed in the prophets' words is "exposed to a ceaseless shattering of indifference, and one needs a skull of stone to remain callous to such blows." The prophets' words are onslaughts that shatter false security rather than general ideas about which one may reflect. Another way of knowing opens up to us in communion with the prophets: our surrender to their impact leads to "moments in which the mind peels off, as it were, its not-knowing" and comprehends by being comprehended. The prophet does not deal, like modern man, with meaninglessness but with deafness to meaning, and the meaning that he speaks is not one of timeless ideas but of the divine understanding of a human situation. Heschel defines prophecy, in fact, as "exegesis of existence from a divine perspective," and he places this exegesis squarely before us as the answer to our own despair: "It is for us to decide whether freedom is self-assertion or response to a demand; whether the ultimate situation is conflict or concern."

7

The Partnership of Existence and the Dialogue of Touchstones

The motto of life is "Give and take." Everyone must be both a giver and a receiver. He who is not both is as a barren tree.

To know the needs of men and to bear the burden of their sorrow — that is the true love of men.[1]

"HUSBAND IS NOT dear because of husband but because of Self within the husband. Wife is not dear because of wife but because of Self within the wife," says the Brihadaranyaka Upanishad. In the non-dualistic (*advaitin*) interpretation of the Hindu Vedanta, this approach to the interpersonal certainly does not exclude furthering the self-realization of the other as well as one's own. But the unity of the two is in the depths of identity, not in the "betweenness" of the relationship. One goes inward to find the Self; one does not find it, except through analogy, in meeting. Uncurtailed personal existence, Buber asserts, is found not in "You over there am I," but in "I accept you as you are":

When taken seriously in the factual, waking continuity of intercourse with one another, the ancient Hindu "That art thou" becomes the postulate of an annihilation of the human person, one's own person as well as the other; for the person is through and through nothing other than uniqueness and thus essentially other than all that is over against it. And even if that supposed universal Self should remain in the ground of the I, it could no longer have intercourse with anyone.

Buber recognizes, of course, that the saying "That art thou" is solely intended in the original teaching for the relation between Brahman and Atman, the Self of being and the self of the human person. Later ages, however, have extended it to the relation between person and person. When this is done, the love between husband and wife serves as a parable of unification but is no longer in itself a touchstone of reality.

> The man who adheres to the teaching of identity may, of course, when he says "Thou" to a fellow man, say to himself in reference to the other, "There are you yourself," for he believes the self of the other to be identical with his. But what the genuine saying of "Thou" to the other in the reality of the common existence basically means — namely, the affirmation of the primally deep otherness of the other, the affirmation of his otherness which is accepted and loved by me — this is devalued and destroyed in spirit through just that identification. The teaching of identity ... contradicts the arch reality of that out of which all community stems — human meeting.[2]

We are confronted here with basic differences in the understanding of reality, meaning, and value that are, in the last instance, religious in nature. Buber makes the above critique in the context of his philosophical anthropology with its teaching that one should, in the words of Heraclitus, "follow the common." No nondualist Vedantist would concern himself with Buber's criticism because for him true "personal" existence and the true *We* of community are found precisely on the road that Buber holds annihilates them. To say this is not to reduce everything to the merely relative, but to recognize a fundamental issue in our understanding of the human.

Early Buddhism held to the teaching of *anatta*, or no self, yet also taught the necessity of the path of the Arhat, the disciple who escapes from the suffering of existence by entering Nirvana. Later Buddhism, especially in the metaphysical doctrines of the Mahayana, denied that there was any individual self to be liberated through entrance into Nirvana while in the popular Mahayana religious ideal the Bodhisattva takes the vow not to enter into Nirvana until *all* sentient beings are delivered from the sufferings of existence. The most awesome exemplar of this vow is the Buddhist monk Santideva. He has been called the Thomas à Kempis of Buddhism, but his goal is actually far broader than his medieval Christian counterpart. While Thomas à Kempis aimed at individual salvation and mystic peace through the imitation of Christ, Santideva aimed at a total practical (not metaphysical) selflessness that has never been surpassed:

> In reward for all this righteousness that I have won by my works, I would fain become a soother of all the sorrows of all creatures. May I be a balm to the sick, their healer and servitor, until sickness come never again; may I quench with rains of food and drink the anguish of hunger and thirst; may I be in the famine of the ages end their drink and meat; may I become an unfailing store for the poor, and serve them with manifold things for their need. My own being and my pleasures, all my righteousness in the past, present, and future, I surrender indifferently, that all creatures may win through to their end. The stillness lies in surrender of all things, and my spirit is fain for the stillness; if I must surrender all, it is best to give it for fellow-creatures. I yield myself to all living things to deal with me as they list; they may smite or revile me for ever, bestrew me with dust, play with my body, laugh and wanton; I have given them my body, why shall I care? Let them make me do whatever works bring them pleasure; but may never mishap befall any of them by reason of me.[3]

The nearest Christian equivalent to this is Saint Francis' prayer:

> O Lord, make me an instrument of Thy peace.
> Where there is hatred, let me sow love
> Where there is injury, pardon
> Where there is doubt, faith

Where there is despair, hope
Where there is darkness, light
Where there is sadness, joy.

O Divine Master
Grant not so much that I seek
To be consoled, as to console
To be understood, as to understand
To be loved, as to love.

The last three lines of the prayer, however, fall short of the spirit of Santideva. In the sublimest sense of the term, they are still self-regarding:

For it is in giving that we receive,
It is in pardoning that we are pardoned,
It is in dying that we are born to Eternal Life.

Lao-tzu too comes surprisingly close to Santideva: "Only he who is willing to give his body for the sake of the world is fit to be entrusted with the world. Only he who can do it with love is worthy of being the steward of the world." Both Lao-tzu and his much later disciple Chuang-tzu understood that "in all human relations, if the two parties are living close to each other, they may form a bond through personal trust." They also understood how words cannot take the place of such personal closeness and trust: "What starts out being sincere usually ends up being deceitful.... Anger arises from no other cause than clever words and one-sided speeches."[4] Lao-tzu, as we have seen, teaches openness to the heart of the other, the flowing interaction of the Tao that leads to what I call "the partnership of existence."

Confucius, too, for all his contrasts with Lao-tzu, pointed to "reciprocity" as the cardinal virtue in the relations between person and person. "Do not do to others what you would not like yourself." He did not, to be sure, understand this as flowing spontaneity but rather as courtesy, consideration, loyalty, respect. Lao-tzu said:

If I keep from meddling with people, they take care of themselves,
If I keep from commanding people, they behave themselves,

If I keep from preaching at people, they improve themselves,
If I keep from imposing on people, they become themselves.

Confucius, in contrast, teaches that real love entails placing a demand on the other for the sake of the relationship: "How can he
be said truly to love, who exacts no effort from the objects of his
love? How can he be said to be truly loyal, who refrains from ad-
monishing the objects of his loyalty?" Confucius was not a strang-
er to the Tao, but he also taught the importance of structure and
propriety, justice and filial loyalty:

> Someone said, What about the saying "Meet resentment
> with inner power [tê]"? The Master said, In that case, how is
> one to meet inner power? Rather meet resentment with up-
> right dealing and meet inner power with inner power.[5]

In the metaphors *the partnership of existence* and *the dialogue of
touchstones* (coined and developed in *Touchstones of Reality*) the
problem of religious communication and that of solitude and community are brought together into a meaningful whole. "We do not
become whole for our own sakes or in terms of ourselves," I wrote
in *Touchstones*. "That is because we *touch* reality at the moment
when we touch what is not ourselves, what calls us, and we bring
ourselves into wholeness from the depths of our being in response
to this call." This is not just a question of the best method of
reaching personal wholeness but of whether our so-called integration can ever properly be considered a goal in itself.

To question this means, of course, to question what to most
people seems self-evident, that we exist primarily for ourselves,
that our chief concern is and should be Me, Number One, *numero
uno*. But it means, equally, to question what most people regard
as the alternative to this position: that altruism in which we deny
ourselves and put ourselves aside for the sake of others. Dietrich
Bonhoeffer has defined Jesus as "the man for others." If we consider Jesus as a man and not as only divine, that is perhaps to give
him too much credit *and* too little. "Father, may this cup be taken
from me," Jesus prayed in the Garden of Gethsemane before his
crucifixion even while he added, "Not my will be done but thine."
If anything is clear from this, it is that Jesus did not *want* to die if

it was not required of him by God *and* that he saw his will as separate from God's though not in conflict.

Pure selfishness is impossible; for we live our lives in relation to others. Pure altruism is also impossible, for we move to meet others from a ground that cannot be denied: the ground of our existence as unique persons, as selves. Much confusion would be cleared up if we distinguished here between the *ego* as the self-regarding, self-involved self, the self that is preoccupied with and aims at itself, and the *I* as that same self when it is not turned back on itself but forgets itself, as it were, in its spontaneous movement to respond to what comes to meet it from the world. No division is implied here such as that of the Hindu Upanishads between the *atman* as some universal or absolute essence of the Self within and the false social self that is totally determined by and imprisoned in the web of social conditioning.

What is meant here was best expressed by the great rabbinic sage Hillel 75 years before Jesus: "If I am not for myself, who will be for me? If I am for myself alone, what am I? And if not now, when?" It is also expressed poignantly in a number of Hasidic tales, when they are held in tension. Rabbi Moshe Leib of Sasov, who used to nurse all the sick boys in the town, said: "He who is not willing to suck the pus from the sore of a child sick with the plague has not climbed even halfway up the mountain to the love of his fellow men." When someone expressed astonishment at his capacity to share in another's troubles, he exclaimed: "What do you mean 'share'? It is my own sorrow; how can I help but suffer it?" On the other hand, when Rabbi Mendel of Rymanov sat in front of his soup without eating it because the servant had forgotten to give him a spoon, his teacher, Rabbi Elimelekh, remonstrated "Look, one must know enough to ask for a spoon, and a plate too, if need be!" Mendel took these words to heart, and from that day on his fortunes were on the mend.

These two seemingly opposite attitudes are brought together in a saying of Yitzhak Eisik of Zhydatchov: "The motto of life is 'Give and take.' Everyone must be both a giver and a receiver. He who is not both is as a barren tree." There are many people who have so resolutely taken on the role of the responsible person or helper that they do not know how to let themselves be helped. Such people tend to end up embittered and "burnt out," for they deny the reality of helping and giving as something that takes place in the between. "As much as the rich man gives the poor man, the poor man gives even more to the rich man." Recognizing what Buber calls the "normative limitation of mutuality" between therapist and client, one psychologist wrote that the only way in which the client can confirm the therapist is in the latter's professional competence. Actually, there is no greater *personal* confirmation that one can give than allowing someone to share in the process of healing or teaching you. Similarly, there is nothing more disconfirming than wanting to heal or teach someone who resolutely refuses to open himself or herself to such partnership!

The whole notion of the social contract that figures so importantly in theories of society from Plato to Hobbes, Rousseau, John Stuart Mill, and Freud, is based on a false split between the individual and society that assumes that persons only relate for the sake of individual benefit. From this standpoint the only mutuality that is possible is that of mutual exploitation, such as Freud's notion of mutual love in which each person finds in the other his or her "cathected love object." If we speak of the partnership of existence, we are suggesting, in contrast, not that people can or should live by some altruistic ideal but that our very existence is only properly understood as a partnership. We become selves *with* one another and live our lives with one another in the most real sense of the term. Put in the language of touchstones of reality, we cannot find reality simply by remaining with ourselves or making ourselves the goal. Paradoxically, we only know ourselves when we know ourselves in responding to others. "By never being an end in himself, he endlessly becomes himself."

At a recent gathering of distinguished philosophers and scientists, I was struck by the tendency of speaker after speaker to substitute for the notion of separate selves the notion that there is only one self. This substitution not only rests on a false dichotomy. It falsifies any possible meaning of the *self*, which cannot be understood adequately either in isolation or as an amalgam of one universal whole. We have to grasp the simplest fact of our existence together, one already hinted at by Plato in the *Symposium*, namely, that we are neither self-sufficient entities nor are we able to come together in such a way as to overcome our separateness and our uniqueness. We are not born a self or an I. We become I in dialogue with other persons whom we meet as persons. This does not imply that we do not exist as a self when we are not with some other person, any more than that in being with another we are automatically in mutual relationship. There is a distinction between our awareness of our self as some sort of continuity *and* our becoming ourselves in the meeting with others — with everything that meets us and calls us out. We must respond to this call from where we are, and where we are is never merely social or merely individual but uniquely personal. We do not begin as isolated consciousness. We need to be confirmed by others. Our very sense of ourselves only comes in this meeting with other selves. Yet through this very meeting we can grow in the strength to respond and to withstand, even though it means, as with Socrates and Jesus, that in the end we must "walk alone."

Those persons whose trust is grounded in the partnership of existence are changed every time they go out to meet another. They become anew and are reborn in each new situation. Obviously, this does not mean total openness without any enduring personal values. The ultimate wisdom combines the structure of Confucius and the spontaneity of Lao-tzu and knows when to stress the one and when the other. We must distinguish between holding our ground and rigidity, even as we must distinguish between going out to meet the other and dissolving the boundaries between person and person in a symbiotic clinging, or what the Gestalt therapists call "confluence." To live means to venture, but it does not mean to give up one's own ground in doing so. There is a difference between openness and self-denial, between risk and suicide. "If I am not for myself, who will be for me? If I am for myself alone, what am I?" How does one know when to emphasize going out and when to emphasize holding one's ground? There is no easy formula. It takes a lifetime to learn the wisdom of responsiveness, the right alternation for this person in this situation between centering oneself and moving out of oneself. What the American poet Theodore Roethke calls "the long journey out of the self" is not achieved by losing touch with oneself any more than it is achieved by aiming at oneself.

Therefore, if we ask the question, "Does the partnership of existence give us 'security' and protect us from tragedy, contradiction, and absurdity?" our answer must be no. There is a basic insecurity in our existence itself that arises from the fact that we cannot live without others and yet often cannot live with them. That is why the psychologist George R. Bok speaks of the necessity of infighting with one's partner in marriage, one's "intimate enemy." Because this insecurity is the human condition, there is an existential anxiety that no amount of psychoanalysis can remove. Again and again, as long as we live, our existence will be endangered by the openness of leaving our ground and the closedness of not leaving it! So far from the partnership of existence excluding tragedy and the absurd, it provides the very ground for them — when meeting becomes mismeeting, when our being face-to-face, or opposite, each other, crystallizes into a fixed and polarized opposition, when the mingling of understanding and misunderstanding that we call communication freezes into the terrifying solitude of the absurd. These are not inevitable expressions of the human condition. They are real events which happen again and again but do not happen necessarily. We are not fundamentally alone. If we were we would not feel lonely. But we again and again find ourselves alone and isolated, "lonely and afraid / in a world I never made." (A. E. Housman).

The loneliness of mismeeting is a real happening, an existential event that may protract into permanence, as happens in some relationships, but *may* also be overcome in deeper meeting. This latter *may* pertains to those situations and relationships in which the partnership of existence proves to have stronger resources than the contradictions and absurdities that pull us apart. We can never know in advance about any particular relationship or situation that this will be so. But we also cannot know that it will *not* be so. Therefore, if we wish to be concrete and realistic, we must try in each situation anew, according to the resources of our persons and of the situation. Applied to the problem of communication, this means that true communication is not a technique but a unique event that may or may not recur, depending upon the commitment to the relationship, the personal resources, the difficulty of the situation, the tension of understanding and misunderstanding. This tension is not greatly relieved if we succeed in agreement on abstract definition of terms, as is customary in the sciences and in logic and mathematics. For in lived speech, it is the way in which we use speech in relationships, including all the nonverbal elements of gesture and mood, that is decisive, not whether the terms we use are different or the same.

Recasting this problem of communication in the language of touchstones of reality will help us grasp it with greater precision and greater depth. The most striking feature of the approach of touchstones is that it substitutes a uniquely personal relation to truth — one that is won by personal responding and contending, by testing and retesting, by reentering the stream of happenings again and again — for an objective, universalist approach to the truth *or* a subjective emotional approach. We are alone with the reality we have found because there is no way to extract it from the event that has produced our touchstone and hand it over to another person. If this be so, then it might seem, at first glance, that while we could communicate about objective matters, any communication of touchstones would be impossible.

This is precisely the view that Søren Kierkegaard takes. Truth, to him, is subjectivity, and communication to him means the forsaking of that subjectivity for objective categories of thought. Kierkegaard understands very well that what is essential to Truth is not the What but the How, but he understands this only in the relation of the "Single One" to God, or the Absolute. As far as the relation between persons is concerned, he warns us to be chary in having to do with one's neighbor and complains of "the wretched tittle-tattle between men that passes for consolation." Putting it another way, Truth for Kierkegaard is dialogical vertically but not horizontally. The "absolute relation to the Absolute" is incompatible with the communication between person and person. "Works of love" result, to be sure, *after* one has become a Single One in relation to God but not during and as an integral part of that process.

Touchstones of reality, in contrast, are dialogical *both* vertically and horizontally, not as if these were two separate dialogues that were somehow conjoined but as a single dialogue in which our contact with the reality of the between arises only in and inseparable from our contact with the existing beings that move to meet us as we them. We are alone with our touchstones, but if they are real — if we have retained them by plowing them back time after time into our lives — the one thing that the other person is sure to meet in any genuine meeting is our touchstones themselves. Touchstones originate in events, and most of the events of our lives are events with others. Touchstones have a two-sidedness that is at the same time a form of immediacy. They are the literal result of our touching on the otherness of the other, and something of that otherness remains with us in any true touchstone even after the contact has ceased to be present. If we must continually go on probing, proving, testing, and authenticating our touchstones, this can only be done in relationship to others and in partnership with them.

Therefore, the very metaphor of touchstones of reality already implies a mutual touching — a touching on the touching of the other, a dialogue of touchstones. Although we cannot say with what we have contact minus the touching, in that very touching we go through and beyond subjective experiencing to a meeting with otherness. "The very act of touching is already a transcending of the self in openness to the impact of something other than the self," I write in "Where Touchstones Meet," the chapter that opens *Touchstones of Reality*. "When two people really touch each other as persons — whether physically or not — the touching is not merely a one-sided impact: it is a mutual revelation of life-stances."

"My soul's been a-witnessin' for the Lord," says a Black spiritual. Ultimately our touchstones are never held in splendid isolation. They are witnesses — the way in which we lace and unlace our felt boots. If we cherish them in our inwardness and do not witness for them with our lives, they atrophy and become mere idea or sentiment rather than lived reality. It is not as if every one of us received his or her touchstones by going into the wilderness like Jacob and dreaming of a ladder stretched between heaven and earth. Many of us find our touchstones in partnership with others, the shared sense of reality of a football team that works well together, the fellowship of friends or even, occasionally, a fraternity or sorority, or the common struggle for a cause that we have made our own. What is more, some of us find our touchstones of reality through our unique response to the touchstones of others as they are communicated to us in a novel, play, or poem, an act of friendship or love, or just the way in which someone lives his or her life.

Of course, our contact with their touchstones is still *our* contact. We do not imitate or take over; we relate to the other's touchstones each in our unique way, and in that unique response a new touchstone of reality comes into being that is the project of our dialogue with the other's touchstone. Therefore, we must still be for ourselves; we must still ask for a spoon and if need be for a plate; we must question and doubt, wrestle and contend. Only after such wrestling will the nameless messenger bless us, as he did Jacob, by giving us a new name, a new touchstone that we can carry with us into life as we go forth to meet *our* Esau — brother and enemy in one. We cannot understand another's touchstone by putting aside ours. We cannot make it our own through empathy or identification. Rather we must "imagine the real," swing over to his or her side, and yet respond with the touchstones we have ourselves brought into our meeting. Hence, the role of objective observer or even of receptive listener will not promote a dialogue of touchstones, but only our willingness to be open *and* to respond personally, from the ground of our own uniqueness.

The touchstones of others, like our own, are personal revelations and witnesses to existential truth. We cannot judge and accept or dismiss them by some objective standard, though we often try to do just that, giving away the fact that we have not really listened to the other at all! We have no right to exclude or deny the other's witness, and neither do we have the right to passively accept and tolerate it. Rather, we must let the other feel that in encountering us he or she is coming up against persons with touchstones and witnesses of their own. Sometimes the strongest opposition is more confirming by far than someone who defends "to the death" your right to your opinion but does not take your touchstone seriously. The real dialogue of touchstones means that we respond from where we are, that we bring ourselves into the dialogue.

If communicating a touchstone means witnessing, then that witness can never be made with words alone. It must always include gestures, actions, pregnant silences, and the reality of the present meeting itself. We cannot share something really unique with unique persons in a unique situation by abstracting from that uniqueness and looking only at the words that are used. As scientists we may build together a conceptual common reality through such abstractions. As persons, we can share the whole of our touchstones and thereby bring what is uniquely our own into a common reality that may even issue into a shared life-stance and, at times, friendship or community.

Therefore, we are not forced to choose between keeping our touchstones to ourselves, and converting them into public knowledge. Touchstones of reality cannot be described or articulated in such a way that they can be objectively handed over, for they always include the fullness of the situation and the component of our unique response to them. John Dewey and Sigmund Freud both rejected mysticism on the ground that it cannot become common public knowledge. Yet from the beginning of human existence, persons have always tried to share with one another events and images that cannot be quantified, defined, or spelled out, but only pointed to. Some of the greatest literature, art, and thought of all ages has been of this nature. "They take the finger pointing to the moon for the moon itself," says the Zen Buddhist of those who forget that religious wisdom is essentially indicative knowledge, a pointer rather than a definer. According to legend, Mahakasyapa became the founder of Zen Buddhism through being the only one to understand when the Buddha silently held up a blue flower in answer to a question!

The dialogue of touchstones excludes models but includes the sharing of uniqueness. "I do exactly as my father did," said one Hasidic rabbi. "He did not imitate, and I do not imitate." We evolve our touchstones in relation to one another; we witness to one another. We have an impact on one another through which we grow in our own touchstones. "Growing in this way," I have claimed, "we come to recognize that a dialogue of touchstones' is itself a touchstone."

Is this not a hopelessly ideal approach in the face of the cultural relativism that reduces our society to a congeries of babbling voices, each asserting itself against the other, each claiming sole truth or denying all truth? Not if we recognize that relativism is only the other side of the same coin as absolutism, that the relativist is the disappointed absolutist who says that if I cannot have one absolute truth, then I shall deny that there is any truth at all. We still long for what Dostoevsky's Grand Inquisitor called the "Unanimous ant heap," a universal religion that will give us the security and comfort of never having to stand our own ground and to think for ourselves.

If we are honest with ourselves, we will recognize that such a universal religion is neither possible nor desirable. The longing for it is a throwback to the desire for a universal, objective Truth that we can possess rather than a touchstone arrived at through obedient listening and faithful responding. If we look dispassionately at the contemporary scene, what is more, we shall recognize that not only are there a great many competing religions that show no slightest trace of merging into one, but also that there are many things that compete with religions for our attention and devotion in such a way that they, too, must be accounted religions in the sense of idols that claim our ultimate allegiance and swallow up our total existence. It little matters whether that idol be money, moloch, magic, materialism, the family, the party, the nation, or even the new world-order.

If we return to the adherents of the religions themselves, we find that the seeming agreement among the members of particular churches and synagogues and religious fellowships is often only illusory. People confess the same faith but mean totally different things by it, or mean nothing at all. How many of us "affirm before the world and deny between the rocks," as T. S. Eliot puts it in "Ash Wednesday"? The fact is that what Abraham Heschel called *religious behaviorism*, the fad of joining for the sake of joining, is so predominant among those who are religious today that it is very difficult in practice to say which particular religious group is what I have called a *community of affinity*, or *like-mindedness* and which is what I have called a *community of otherness*. The former is a pseudo-community based on the false security of commonly-ascribed-to catchphrases or the equally false security of belonging just for the sake of belonging and promoting the religious institution as an end in itself. The latter is the fellowship of really other persons brought together in the struggle for a common cause, one to which they relate from unique perspectives and life-stances yet which they share and find real fellowship in that sharing.

The true fellowship of the committed who can meet and talk with one another because they really care about one another and the common goal they are serving, however differently that goal may be stated, is often found not within but *across* organizational, institutional, and denominational lines. It is my experience that I can talk to a committed person of any religion or even no religion at all better than I can talk to an uncommitted person of my own religion so long as that commitment does not fall into the idolatry of objectifying one's touchstones into universal truths that one wishes to impose upon others and force everyone to ascribe to. If this is so, then the answer to the dilemma of cultural relativism is not a new universalism or a new absolutism, nor even some "perennial philosophy" that claims to have found the true essence of all religions, but a faithful pluralism — a mutually confirming dialogue of touchstones.

What I am talking about is not an attitude confined to individuals. It may be represented in a group itself, as in The Working Party for the Future of the Quaker Movement, to which I belonged for four years, not as a Quaker but as a Jew. My closeness or distance from the others was not determined by this nomenclature but by the very individual touchstones and life-stances of the members, some of whom could not affirm the divinity of Christ and some of whom could not do without that affirmation, some of whom were mystics and some of whom were not, some of whom were concerned with group process and others who were totally turned off by that concern. One of the things that I witness to in my chapter on The Working Party in *Touchstones of Reality* is that we do not need to use the same words as others or even to affirm that beneath our different words and images we really mean the same thing in order to share a meaningful religious fellowship.

In contrast to those like Aldous Huxley, Henri Bergson, and Erich Fromm, who have proclaimed a perennial philosophy that obliterates essential differences, we can accept the fact that we not only have different paths but also that these different paths may lead to different places. What matters is that in listening to the other we hear something genuine to which we can respond. Real religious fellowship does not begin with creed or catechism but with genuine trust. We receive from each other without ever being identical with each other; we are able to affirm and respond to what we receive, and grow through it. Some religions, to be sure, seek to articulate abstract criteria of faith and creed. But unless those abstractions are rooted in lived tradition and lived community of trust, they are worthless. On the other hand, even the silence of a gathered Quaker meeting, which dispenses with all concepts, should not deceive its members into thinking they have attained unity during the meeting. The most we can responsibly speak of is community and communion, which enable the members of a fellowship to be really different and yet really together.

The dialogue of touchstones is not between religions but between persons and groups. For all that we speak of Jewish-Christian dialogue, for example, it is always, in fact, only particular Jews and particular Christians who are in dialogue and never the religions as such. That becomes self-evident as soon as we recall that dialogue only takes place between persons. Religions and religious institutions, whatever else they may be, are not persons! There has thrived in our day, unfortunately, a form of pseudo-dialogue in which official representatives of religions carry on official dialogues that are neither genuine meetings of religions, for religions cannot meet, nor genuine meetings of persons because these persons speak only for their social role and do not stand behind what they say with their own persons.

On the other hand, there is a new spirit of openness abroad among many religious thinkers. Real listening is already a form of responding, and real response is not only dialogue but sharing from a different side in a common reality. Once in a discussion with an eminent Catholic theologian, I asserted that even after Vatican II Judaism could not be expected to enter fully into dialogue with Catholicism because the Church still claims to have superseded the people of the covenant as the "true Israel." His complete agreement with what I said was an honest recognition of difference that was already a step toward overcoming it.

Many share the illusion that if people could just arrive at the same terms, they would be in real communication and agreement. Actually, no real communication takes place except by one person speaking from one vantage point and the other listening and responding from a really other vantage point — the ground of his uniqueness. My word is a part of my witness. I cannot give it up. But I wish to witness to *you*. Therefore, I cannot impose my word on you. I want you to hear and respond to it *from your side* rather than passively to accept it. All I can legitimately ask of you is to listen to me and to be actively what you are in response to me.

If this is so, then we cannot have the notion of "one truth" of which our individual truths are so many symbolic expressions. Every one of us has to witness from where he or she is. We shall never find a common philosophy, theology, or myth that unites us. But we can share our myths with one another and grow in the strength to live without a single, all-encompassing myth. We can distinguish here between the myths of process, evolution, or the unconscious that *we* possess and the myth that possesses and lives us, the totally nonobjectifiable myth of the Community of Otherness. This "metamyth" removes the very desire for a common myth; for it holds us together, borne in a common stream. This unarticulable myth is perhaps greater than any myth that can only be lived out in the lives of individuals. Wherever persons of no-matter-what religion, or none at all, meet in a spirit of common concern, ready to encounter each other beyond their terminologies, the metamyth of the Community of Otherness can come into being and with it the lived reality of community.

The ultimate issue and goal of the dialogue of touchstones is not communication, therefore, but community — lived togetherness of really unique persons, families, and groups. True community comes into being not through tolerance but through mutual confirmation. No group is able to confirm all otherness. That is beyond human capacity. But the test of a fellowship is the otherness that it can confirm. To begin with, a group ought not to go out to gather other people in but should try to understand from within the actual people that are already present.

If the spokesman of the group explains to someone who differs with him that he is not really a member of the group because he does not fit the former's conception of the group, he will not only have read him out of the group, but out of existence itself as far as this moment and this situation are concerned. The obverse attitude is that of openness and trust. It is our lack of trust, our existential mistrust, that makes us feel that we have to have the security of like-minded groups, groups based on generalized affinity, rather than the concreteness of open meeting with real otherness that is present in every group, down to a pair of friends or a husband and wife.

The Community of Otherness might serve as a model for the dialogue of all persons in contemporary culture — a way of being faithful and diverse at the same time. Many people feel that we have to choose between an exclusivist truth and a hopeless relativism. The half-truth in this is that, for most of us, the appeal to unanimity and universality is a thing of the past. We live in dialogue with other individuals and peoples with different faiths, cultures, and values than our own, and even within our own cultures and faiths there is today often more variety than there is homogeneity. The half-falsehood is that the relativism that seems to deny universality is, in fact, the sickness of universalism turned inside out. It does not accept things as they happen in their *uniqueness*, for it knows only *difference* — comparison and contrast in terms of categories. In contrast to the either/or of absolutism and relativism, I offer as a genuine and more fruitful third alternative the mutual confirmation of the dialogue of touchstones.

We should also give up the notion that some persons possess the spirit and others do not. The spirit that speaks through us is a response to the spirit that we meet in others, the spirit that meets us in the between. This spirit may express itself in silence or in words or in both. The words that are spoken *out* of the silence of a fellowship bear witness to a gathered presence that transcends the particular set of words that each member of the fellowship may use. This gathered presence gropes toward and responds to the diversity of individuals without aiming at any final answers or conclusions.

We live our lives in a movement between immediacy and objectification. What matters is not the one or the other taken by itself, but the spirit that leads us from the one to the other and back again. This spirit does not stand in contrast to words. It finds its true life in the encounter of words when that encounter means caring and concern, in the contending of words when that contending means witnessing and confirming. Our ultimate concerns touch one another through and beyond all words. This going *through* the word to a meeting *beyond* the word can be a more powerful witness to the imageless God than any dogma, creed, theology, or metaphysic.

In the "Disputations in Religion" section of his essay "Dialogue," Martin Buber gives powerful witness to this understanding of human words and the Word of God within the dialogue of touchstones:

> I have not the possibility of judging Luther, who refused fellowship with Zwingli in Marburg, or Calvin who furthered the death of Servetus. For Luther and Calvin believe that the Word of God has so descended among men that it can be clearly known and must therefore be exclusively advocated. I do not believe that; the Word of God crosses my vision like a falling star by whose fire the meteorite will bear witness without making it light up for me, and I myself can only bear witness to the light but not produce the stone and say "This is it." But this difference of faith is by no means to be understood merely as a subjective one. It is not based on the fact that we who live to-day are weak in faith, and it will remain even if our faith is ever so much strengthened. The situation of the world itself, in the most serious sense, more precisely the relation between God and man, has changed. And this change is certainly not comprehended in its essence by our thinking only of the darkening, so familiar to us, of the supreme light, only of the

night of our being, empty of revelation. It is the night of an expectation — not of a vague hope, but of an expectation. We expect a theophany of which we know nothing but the place, and the place is called *community*. In the public catacombs of this expectation there is no single God's Word which can be clearly known and advocated, but the words delivered are clarified for us in our human situation of being turned to one another. There is no obedience to the coming one without loyalty to his creature. To have experienced this is our way.

A time of genuine religious conversations is beginning — not those so-called but fictitious conversations where none regarded and addressed his partner in reality, but genuine dialogues, speech from certainty to certainty, but also from one open-hearted person to another open-hearted person. Only then will genuine common life appear, not that of an identical content of faith which is alleged to be found in all religions, but that of the situation, of anguish and of expectation.[6]

Part four

The Tension
Between Past and Present

8

Peter Pan's Shadow:
Tradition and Modernity

WE CANNOT FIND touchstones of reality by going *back* to tradition. We can only find them through renewing tradition, through making it living again in the present. "Not our fathers, but we here, the living, stand on Mount Sinai to receive the Covenant." This does not mean that there is no difference or tension between our fathers and us. "Over an abyss of sixteen hundred years I speak to you," says Saint Nicholas at the beginning of Benjamin Britten's *St. Nicholas Cantata*. If we attempt to continue tradition without the awareness of this abyss, without holding the tension between the traditional and the contemporary, we lose the tension that makes such handing down, the original meaning of *tradition*, fruitful. Only when we have three elements — our personal uniqueness, the will to be open, and holding the tension with tradition — is there a meaningful dynamic. We must fight and contend with tradition in order to make an honest witness to our own uniqueness *and* to all the absurdity and incongruity that has entered into our lives.

If cutting ourselves off from tradition is one danger, there is an equal danger in retaining the time-hallowed symbols yet reading into them new meaning so freely that, like Peter Pan's shadow, it is sewed onto the old. "Forms in themselves are nothing," Martin Buber has said, once they have been cut off from their origin, that which pervaded them as the soul pervades the body. "Once they have grown empty, one cannot fill them with a new, timely content; they will not hold it. Once they have decayed, they cannot be resuscitated by infusion with a spirit other than their own." The most glaring example I know of this arbitrary transvaluation of religious symbols is the Reconstructionist philosophy of Mordecai Kaplan, one of the most significant and influential of contemporary Jewish theologians.

Basing his own thought on the evolutionary naturalism of John Dewey and others, Kaplan offers a conscious reevaluation of Judaism in place of the unconscious ones that have been effectuated in the past to resolve the tension between tradition and the thought of the time (Aristotle, Plato, Kant, or the universalism of the Enlightenment, to name a few). Kaplan's strength lies in the honesty with which he has set the problem of how to bring the Jewish tradition into vital relation with the modern world, in his recognition of the importance of the Jewish people, civilization, and culture, in his opening the way to fuller identification with Judaism for the modern American Jew, and his correction of the unduly abstract, universalist tendencies of nineteenth-century Reform Judaism. Kaplan defines Judaism as "a religious civilization" —

> the ensemble of the following organically interrelated elements of culture: a feeling of belonging to a historic and indivisible people, rootage in a common land, a continuing history, a living language and literature, and common mores, laws and arts, with religion as the integrating and soul-giving factor of all these elements.[1]

That religion really is the "integrating and soul-giving factor" in Kaplan's view is called into question, however, by his further statement that "the 'Torah' or Israel's way of life, represents culture" whereas "'The Holy One' represents religion," which must itself be reinterpreted "so that it can be rendered compatible with a reasonable conception of naturalism."

In Kaplan's basic theological work, *The Meaning of God in*

Modern Jewish Religion (1936), God becomes either identical with the aspirations and values of human, or Jewish, civilization, or he becomes the instrumentality through which they are fulfilled — a type of creative cosmic force that guarantees that nature is so constituted that this fulfillment is inevitable. In his reevaluation of Judaism in *The Meaning of God*, Kaplan retains a series of terms, each of which, *by its very meaning* quite as much as by its traditional usage, implies relation to *otherness* and to *transcendence*, and makes them all immanent. Holiness, Judgment, Atonement, Sovereignty, Kingship, Covenant, Salvation — each in turn is arbitrarily converted into self-realization, significance, values, creative force, organic growth, evolution. What we are left with is an impossible dualism in which the outer form is provided by tradition, the inner meaning by modern culture. To "love the Lord thy God with all thy heart, soul, mind, and might" becomes seeking God in all of life, and seeking God Kaplan defines in modern Platonic as investigating "truth, beauty, goodness" to their utmost reaches. This dualism of outer form and inner meaning is perhaps more of a threat to the survival of Judaism or any other religion than an aid. The traditional structures and shapes of all religions have developed out of the religious reality of that religion as it has been imprinted in cultural and social forms and cannot be separated from that origin without destroying the vital relationship of the worshiper to the primordial religious reality that again and again gives rise to the form. To preserve them with an entirely new, so-called modern meaning, pinned on like Peter Pan's shadow, is to preserve them in name only. In fact, not only the relationship to the form and hence its meaning, but the form itself will change in accordance with the actual meaning it has for the modern worshiper.

In *The Future of an American Jew* (1948), Kaplan equates faith in God with a striving for self-fulfillment in conformity with the conditions inherent in the nature of the universe. Yet on the next page he defines "the religious element in a people's civilization as institutions, places, historic events, popular heroes, and other objects of popular reverence to which superlative importance or sanctity is ascribed." Not only is the fact of the people's holding these important sufficient to make them *sancta*, but there is no difference between the *sancta* of Judaism, such as the Sabbath and the Prophets, and the *sancta* of the American nation, such as the Fourth of July and the Stars and Stripes. These latter "represent American religion" to which the American Jew presumably owes equal reverence along with the God of Judaism! Where in all this is there still a discernible religious element or room for a prophetic protest against the idolatry of nationalism? "Whatever a civilization values highly it views as, in some measure, a manifestation of God in Human life." The revelation of God becomes identical with the prospering of human affairs: "Even where God is not consciously felt or identified, He nevertheless functions through those aspects of man's environment and inner life which make for man's security, welfare and spiritual growth."

Most baffling of all is Kaplan's combination of Jewish peoplehood as the core of Judaism with universal values in terms of which Judaism is to be reinterpreted. "Ritual and religious symbolism are the main technique for effecting 'consciousness of kind' among Jews," writes Kaplan. A rite or symbol has value for Judaism quite as much "if it makes us Israel-conscious" as if it makes us "God-conscious." Yet "one of the main tasks of Jewish religion of the future" is "to reinterpret the classic cultural heritage of the Jewish past from the viewpoint of our modern this-worldly and universal concept of salvation." "The distinctiveness of Jewish religion must not appear in any difference of aim between it and other ethical religions." "Any ideal that is of universal significance, that belongs not to the worship of Power but of Spirit, is capable of adoption by, and adaptation to, any and all religious traditions." Here again we have an impossible dualism — between a particular religious tradition and universal values which exist independently of that tradition and are applied to it!

In the end, like ethical humanism, Kaplan takes for granted both the source and the resources of moral values, defining religion pragmatically as "a dynamic response to man's need to give meaning to his life" and the "Torah of the Lord" functionally as "whatever is perfect and restores the soul" (*A New Zionism*, 1955). *Questions Jews Ask* (1956) is replete with this same pragmatic inversion of biblical Judaism: "To make for the good life, the God of Israel is assumed to have revealed to His people the Torah. . . . To hold out hope for the future, God is conceived as certain to send the Messiah for Israel's redemption." Though we cannot demonstrate the correctness of the assumption that the universe is congenial or favorable to human fulfillment, "we hold to it, because it is indispensable to mental health and the sense of moral responsibility." "Without faith in God, in this sense, there can be no valid ethics, because without it, one can find no rationale for that measure of self-sacrifice and self-transcendence which is indispensable for ethical living." In other words, we do not know that God exists — *even in Kaplan's sense* of Cosmic Process, a "Power not ourselves that makes for righteousness" — yet we must act *as if* he exists in order that we may have a rationale for ethical living. But the person who rejects self-sacrifice and self-transcendence will hardly be moved by Kaplan's appeal to retain them for the sake of "ethical living," for that person will reject "ethical living" too! William James to the contrary, one cannot will to believe *just in order to attain* beneficial results. Either there *is* meaning in life that can be discovered in our meeting with reality, or there is not. There is no meaning "As If."

Evolutionary naturalism is not the only form in which contemporary thinkers have tired to sew Peter Pan's shadow onto traditional religious values and institutions in our day. While Freud may have dismissed religion as the "illusion" of our ignorant ancestors, many of our contemporaries have followed Erich Fromm, C. G. Jung, and others in reinstating religion with a whole new set of immanentist psychological values in which religion, instead of becoming a function of natural process or ethical living, becomes a function of humanist psychology or the individuation of the person.

Erich Fromm represents a halfway point between Mordecai Kaplan and Carl Jung because his universalist approach to religion is deeply rooted, like Kaplan's, in traditional Judaism and because he, too, espouses a humanistic naturalism, albeit a psychological and somewhat mystical one. The nature of an individual's love for God corresponds to the nature of his love for man, states Fromm. But this is hardly true for Fromm himself, whose usual recognition of the otherness of the other party in the healthy mature relationship between person and person entirely disappears in his various discussions of religion. In human relations, Fromm affirms the self *and* the other and denies that one must choose between self-love and love of others. In religion Fromm posits the self *or* the other, denying *a priori* the possibility that man may "fulfill himself" in relation to what transcends him. In both spheres, however, he allows a pragmatic motif to dominate in a spirit very similar to that of Mordecai Kaplan. He defines ethics in terms of what produces a mature, integrated personality, and he defines religion in the same extrinsic way. *Good* and *bad* in religion, as in ethics, are functions of the psychological effect of a type of relationship rather than of any intrinsic value or disvalue in the relationship itself. What matters to the psychologist, writes Fromm in *Psychoanalysis and Religion*, is what human attitude a religion expresses and what kind of effect it has on man, whether it is good or bad for the development of man's powers.

"Authoritarian religion," according to this formula, is bad, and therefore presumably untrue, because in it man projects his own powers on a transcendent God and crushes himself under a burden of guilt and sin. His only access to himself is through God, whom he must beg to return some of what was originally his own.Completely at God's mercy, he feels himself a sinner, without faith in his fellow men or in himself. Incapable of love, he tries in vain to recover some of his lost humanity by being in touch with God. "The more he praises God, the emptier he becomes. The emptier he becomes, the more sinful he feels. The more sinful he feels, the more he praises God — and the less able is he to regain himself."

Fromm's category of *authoritarian religion* is somewhat more recognizable, even in his caricature of it, than his category of *humanistic religion*. Like Aldous Huxley, Fromm presents us with a perennial philosophy — "a core of ideas and norms" common to the teachings of "Lao-tse, Buddha, the Prophets, Socrates, Jesus, Spinoza, and the philosophers of the Enlightenment." This common core Fromm describes as striving to recognize the truth, being independent and free, relating to one's fellow men lovingly, knowing the difference between good and evil, and learning to listen to the voice of one's conscience. The variegated assortment of religions and philosophies Fromm lists as humanistic may all affirm man, but they do so in such contrasting ways as to make their similarities less important than their differences.

One need only contrast biblical Judaism and Hasidism with Spinoza and the Enlightenment to see immediately that Fromm's either/or of transcendent versus immanent religion is entirely inadequate. A third category of transcendence-immanence, of man in dialogue with God, of the self *and* the reality over against it, is necessary to do justice to biblical and Hasidic Judaism, much of Christian and Sufi mysticism, Hindu Bhakti, or devotional religion, and a large part of Mahayana Buddhism. Fromm characterizes humanistic religion as "centered around man and his strength," developing the power of reason, experiencing the solidarity of all living beings, experiencing "oneness with the All," achieving the greatest strength and realizing the self. "Inasmuch as humanistic religions are theistic, God is a symbol of *man's own powers* which he tries to realize in his life." But Job did not look on the God with whom he contended as "a symbol of man's own powers," nor did St. Francis or the Baal-Shem-Tov remove their God from a reality over-against them to a potentiality within them. To interpret them in this way is fundamentally to distort them.

In contrast to Freud and even Fromm, Carl G. Jung is open to every variety and manifestation of religion. So far from considering religion an illusion, Jung finds in the religions of mankind the golden ore which, when it is extracted and refined, becomes the alchemist's stone not only of healing but of personal integration and spiritual fulfillment. Jung's approach to religion and psychology is *gnostic* in its concern for saving knowledge, in its attitude toward the unification of good and evil, and in its pointing toward an élite of those who have attained individuation and got beyond the relativity of good and evil. It is *modern* in the fact that none of the Gnostic symbols Jung uses have the transcendent value that they originally possessed but all stand for transformations and processes within the psyche, shading as that does, for Jung, into a vast, collective, and essentially autonomous area that is reached through, but is not dependent upon, the individual conscious ego or even the personal unconscious.

If to Jung the Christian symbol is gnosis and the compensation of the unconscious still more so, his gnosis is rooted in the psyche, and it is psychic experience that is expressed in Jung's *gnostic* myth. In *Psychology and Alchemy*, Jung sees Christ as not only *not condemning* the sinner but also as *espousing* him. The medieval alchemists preferred "to seek through knowledge rather than to find through faith," and in this "they were in much the same position as modern man, who prefers immediate personal experience to belief in traditional ideas." If Jung here again equates knowledge with personal experience, he is still more modern in asserting that "the central ideas of Christianity are rooted in Gnostic philosophy, which, in accordance with psychological laws, simply *had* to grow up at a time when the classical religions had become obsolete." Jesus becomes the great prototype of the Modern Gnostic:

> There have always been people who, not satisfied with the dominants of conscious life, set forth ... to seek direct experience of the eternal roots, and, following the lure of the restless unconscious psyche, find themselves in the wilderness where, like Jesus, they come up against the son of darkness.[2]

In *Aion* Jung asserts that the totality of the self is indistinguishable from the God image. Jung substitutes for Christ's teaching of *perfection* the archetypal teaching of *completeness*, which he identifies with Paul's confession, "I find then a law, that, when I would do good, evil is present with me." What Paul lamented, Jung affirms, namely, the experiencing of evil within oneself:

> Only the "complete" person knows how unbearable man is to himself. So far as I can see, no relevant objection could be raised from the Christian point of view against anyone accepting the task of individuation imposed on us by nature, and the recognition of our wholeness or completeness, as a binding personal commitment.[3]

Gnostic salvation of the soul in relation to the transcendent

God is now equated with bringing the warring opposites of the conscious and unconscious into "a healthier and quieter state (salvation)." Though the history of the Gnostic symbol of the *anima mundi* or Original Man "shows that it was always used as a God-image," we may assume, says Jung, "that some kind of psychic wholeness is meant (for instance, conscious + unconscious)." "I have not done violence to anything," Jung finds it necessary to explain. Psychology establishes "that the symbolism of psychic wholeness coincides with the God-image." The Gnostics possessed the idea of an unconscious — the same knowledge as Jung's — "formulated differently to suit the age they lived in." To say that "each new image is simply another aspect of the divine mystery immanent in all creatures" is absolutely synonymous to Jung with saying that "all these images are found empirically to be expressions for the unified wholeness of man."

Instead of seeing the Gnostics as they for the most part were — enormously abstruse system-builders and mythicizers — Jung turns them into modern thinkers, "theologians who, unlike the more orthodox ones, allowed themselves to be influenced in large measure by natural inner experience." The Gnostic dissolution of Christ's personality into symbols for the kingdom of God is praised by Jung as representing "an assimilation and integration of Christ into the human psyche" through which human personality grows and consciousness develops. "By making the person of Christ the object of his devotions," claims Jung, man "gradually came to acquire Christ's position as mediator."

God is completely identified by Jung with individuated man, and the new mystery that he proclaims is the mystery of God become man.

> A modern mandala is an involuntary confession of a peculiar mental condition. There is no deity in the mandala, nor is there any submission or reconciliation to a deity. *The place of the deity seems to be taken by the wholeness of man.*
>
> If we want to know what happens when the idea of God is no longer projected as an autonomous entity, this is the answer of the unconscious psyche. *The unconscious pro-*

duces the idea of a deified or divine man.

The goal of psychological, as of biological, development is self-realization, or individuation. But since man knows himself only as an ego, and the self, as a totality, is indescribable and indistinguishable from a God-image, *self-realization* — to put it in religious or metaphysical terms — *amounts to God's incarnation.*[4]

The remarkable thing about these statements is that Jung sees no essential difference between man's relation to the inner self and ancient man's relation to the divine other. Jung ascribes certain qualities of otherness to the archetypal unconscious, to be sure, in particular that sense of numinous awe of which Rudolph Otto has spoken. But he has robbed his commanding voice of the essential otherness by identifying it with one's own destiny, one's law, one's daimon, one's creativity, one's true self, one's life-will. For this "voice" never comes from the other that one meets (other people are seen by Jung as projections of one's own anima or animus) but from within. While Jung may retain a certain amount of inverted divine transcendence or wholly otherness in his view of the transpersonal objective psyche, he rules out of *primary* consideration as revelation and command the life between person and person. Jung's ineffable and unconscious "objective psyche" is other than one's conscious ego and even one's personal unconscious, but it is not other than the self in the larger and more complete sense in which Jung uses that term. Nor is it other in the sense in which I am really other than you, however overwhelming the universal psyche may be. Therefore, it seems to me a misuse of terms when some of Jung's followers suggest that one relates to the objective psyche as Thou. The mutuality of the I-Thou relationship that enabled Abraham and Job to contend with God seems to be entirely lacking in Jung's understanding of the relation between the personal ego and personal unconscious, on the one hand, and the objective psyche on the other.

If anything, the collective unconscious, or objective psyche, is a more basic and all-inclusive reality to Jung than is God. God too is a "psychic reality like the unconscious," an archetype that already has its place in that part of the psyche that is preexistent to the consciousness. This gives God, and the other archetypes, an autonomy from the conscious mind, but they are nonetheless psychic. Although Jung does not claim that a God that cannot be known in the psyche does not exist, he says that for all practical purposes such a God does not exist because we can know the existence of only what is psychic.

> The conception of God as an autonomous psychic content makes God into a moral problem — and that, admittedly, is very uncomfortable. But if this problem does not exist, God is not real, for where can he touch our lives. He is then either an historical and intellectual bogey or a philosophical sentimentality.[5]

In *Answer to Job*, Jung's psychologism reaches the absurd length of psychoanalyzing God. "From the human point of view Yahweh's behavior is so revolting," he writes, "that one has to ask oneself whether there is not a deeper motive hidden behind it. Has Yahweh some secret resistance against Job?" According to Jung, "he pays so little attention to Job's real situation that one suspects him of having an ulterior motive which is more important to him." Jung sees God, indeed, as projecting his shadow side "with brazen countenance" and "remaining unconscious at man's expense." Even Freud never took so literally the unmasking of motives characteristic of psychological man! In *Answer to Job* Jung rejects the charge of psychologism on the curious grounds that he regards the psyche as *real* — and then offers abundant evidence that the charge is justly made. That he falls into the logical error of seeing reality as *either* physical or psychic is clear from such statements as "God is an obvious psychic and non-physical fact, i.e., a fact that can be established psychically but not physically," and "Religious statements without exception have to do with the reality of the psyche and not with the reality of physis."

The only action that Jung recognizes as real is from the unconscious and never from any independently other person or reality. Hence he states, "God acts out of the unconscious of man"; "It is only through the psyche that we can establish that God acts upon us"; and "Only that which acts upon me do I recognize as real and actual." Even the Holy Scriptures are "utterances of the soul," and God is indistinguishable from the unconscious, or more exactly from the archetype of the self within the unconscious. Like many ancient Gnostics, Jung begins by distorting the imageless God of the Old Testament into the evil Creator God. Only a *Modern* Gnostic, however, could hold this god to be a projection of the collective unconscious of mankind, as Jung does, and yet rant at it in a highly personal manner. "Yahweh displays no compunction, remorse, or compassion, but only ruthlessness and brutality. The plea of unconsciousness is invalid, seeing that he flagrantly violates at least three of the commandments he himself gave out on Mount Sinai." God, to Jung, is not conscious, and is therefore not man. Yet he is seen by Jung as conscious enough to be aware that he is inferior to man and at the same time human enough to be personally jealous!

God, for Jung, is the "loving Father" who is unmasked as dangerous, unpredictable, unreliable, unjust, and cruel, in short "an insufferable incongruity which modern man can no longer swallow." The essential content of the unconscious, writes Jung, is *the idea of the higher man* by whom Yahweh is morally defeated and whom he was later to become." Man not only judges God, in Jung's reading; he ultimately replaces him. The apocalyptic writers such as Ezekiel foresee "what is going to happen through the transformation and humanization of God, not only to God's son as foreseen from all eternity, but to man as such." The incarnation of God in Christ is not enough; for Christ is perfect man but not complete, i.e., sinful man. The new incarnation will be that of God in sinful man. "*God will be begotten in creaturely man.*"

This, Jung quite rightly remarks, "implies a tremendous change in man's status, for he is now raised to sonship and almost to the position of a man-god." The deification of man as "man-god" that Dostoevsky foresaw as the abysmal consequence of "the death of God" is now openly hailed by Jung. "*God wanted to become man and still wants to.*"

From the promise of the Paraclete we may conclude that God wants to become *wholly* man; in other words, to reproduce himself in his own dark creature (man not re-deemed from original sin). God ... wants to become man, and for that purpose he has chosen, through the Holy Ghost, the creaturely man filled with darkness — the natur-al man who is tainted with original sin and who learnt the divine arts and sciences from the fallen angels. The guilty man is eminently suitable and is therefore chosen to be-come the vessel for the continuing incarnation, not the guiltless one who holds aloof from the world and refuses to pay his tribute to life, for in him the dark God would find no room.[6]

Man now unites the light and dark, the good and evil of the di-vine in himself. Man "has been granted an almost godlike power": he must know God's nature "if he is to understand him-self and thereby achieve gnosis of the Divine."

Jung sees no middle ground between sinless man and sinful man, no possibility of sinful man transforming and hallowing his instincts rather than simply celebrating and integrating them. By identifying the real self with the autonomous center in the un-conscious, Jung is in danger of taking his own inner knowledge for the will of God and imposing it upon others. That Jung may not entirely have escaped from this danger is suggested by his celebration in *Answer to Job* of the new Roman Catholic dogma of the Assumption of Mary. He considers this dogma "to be the most important religious event since the Reformation" — not be-cause of any of the reasons that the Catholic Church would hold to be important, but because it gives the feminine principle the place in the deity that Jung's psychology calls for![7]

Freud has retained of religion the superstitious terror and the propitiation of the angry father. Fromm has retained of religion all this *plus* the very real humanistic values he finds in a variety of religions and philosophies. Jung has retained the uncanny, numinous dread of religion, its overwhelming power, man's sense of creatureliness and his possibilities of ecstasy. But none of the three has been able to allow religion to speak with its own voice and in its own terms. All three have transferred it, each ac-cording to his own notion of the psyche, claiming thereby to have arrived at the true essence beneath the surface appearance.

Religion that is not taken at face value but reduced to what it "really is" is no more truly met than the person whose stated words and conscious intentions one entirely dismisses in favor of one's own "insight" into the workings of the other's unconscious.

In the chapter on "Psychology and Religion" in *Touchstones of Reality* I make a distinction that is usually ignored between psychlogy *of* religion and psychology *and* religion. Psychology *of* religion uses religion as the material for its thought, but it takes the form and meaning from the categories and insights of psychology. Psychology *and* religion envisages a meeting on equal terms between two essentially different realities: a body of knowledge within the structure of a science and a body of tradition, ritual, history, and experience accessible in parts to many sciences and as a whole to none.

The meeting of psychology and religion brings to light the *limits* of the psyche as touchstones of reality. Many today take psychology or the psyche for granted as the ultimate court of appeal as to what is real. For them, the question of touchstones of reality in the immediate and concrete sense in which the touchstones derive from concrete encounters or events can hardly arise:

> Today the psychological in the sense of objective analysis and the psychic in the sense of subjective experience are confusedly intermingled. Yet this confused intermingling has taken shape in the popular mind not only as a single phenomenon but as *the* modern touchstone of reality in the way theology was for the Middle Ages, physics for the Newtonian age and the age of Enlightenment, and evolution for the mid-nineteenth to mid-twentieth centuries. Here I am using the phrase "touchstone of reality" in a derivative, objectified, and cultural sense rather than in an existential sense as a product of some direct encounter or contact with an otherness that transcends our own subjectivity even when we respond to it from that ground.[8]

The two senses of touchstones of reality that I distinguish in the "Psychology and Religion" chapter of *Touchstones* can help us understand in greater depth the problem of tradition and modernity. These two senses are often quite distinct, but seldom entirely so, for we live in culture, and our contacts with any reality whatever are refracted through culture — including language, concepts, and world-views; ways of seeing, thinking, and experiencing, and attitudes and expectations. Nonetheless, I do not believe that we are entirely determined by our social constructions of reality, as some modern sociologists of religion seem to hold. It is not that we can escape from culture or the social, but that our relationship to it differs depending upon whether we are merely shaped by it or bring our own unique response to it. If there is no contact with reality that is wholly separate from culture, there *is* culture that is far removed from any direct contact with reality. In this latter case, our "touchstones" become both obstacles to and substitutes for any immediacy of apprehension or reapprehension of the reality known in mutual contact.

In speaking of the widespread popular tendency to make the psyche the *cultural* touchstone of reality, I am not suggesting that Freud, Fromm, or Jung failed to develop touchstones of their own based on the immediate encounters and events of their lives. I am speaking, rather, of the authority with which psychology has been invested in our age, as theology and philosophy were in other ages. There has *always* been a problem of tradition and modernity, for tradition is an organically growing and changing phenomenon, and all great religions have witnessed the passing on of religious insights and teachings to people whose land, culture, language, and life-conditions were vastly different from those among whom the religion originally arose. What is different about our contemporary problem of tradition and modernity is, first, that for many psychology has taken the place that philosophy, theology, or the physical and biological sciences held in other ages. Second, contemporary thinkers and seekers are exposed to a vast array of conflicting and interacting cultures, philosophies, psychologies, and religious traditions, which often leads to universalist formulations rather than to that mutually confirming pluralism for which I call. Third, the tension between religion and science and the triumph of secularism have led many to a *conscious* reevaluation that accomplishes the transvaluation of meaning that in past ages took place unconsciously.

The object of my critique of Kaplan, Fromm, and Jung has not been to disparage their thought in itself, but to show how each illustrates, in a quite different way, the problem of "Peter Pan's shadow" — the attempt to sew modern meanings onto ancient tradition in a fairly arbitrary way that leaves us with an impossible dualism between form and content. Our concern with the limits of the psyche as touchstone of reality does not imply that it is illegitimate for a psychologist to express his or her views on religion. What we are focusing on here, rather, is the tendency to bolster these new insights by recasting them in old forms, putting new wine into old skins. Kaplan does this through holding onto the rituals and traditions of Judaism while reinterpreting them in terms of naturalist, evolutionary, and universalist meanings. Fromm and Jung, in contrast, wed their thinking to no one religion, though Fromm originally stems from Judaism and Jung consistently applies his thought to a radical reinterpretation of Christianity.

Do not other theologians and philosophers of religion reinterpret and reevaluate? Of course. For tradition is a dialogue, and there is no way that we can bring ourselves into identity with the founders of a tradition. Yet the necessity of responding from where we are can be done with full consciousness of the tension between the present and the past and of the difficulty of making the past living again in the present. Or it can be done without faithfulness to the original tradition in such a way that the tensions are covered over and sleight-of-hand reinterpretations are introduced in the name of harmonizing ancient religion and modern thought. I once went to a Reform Jewish Seder service on the first night of Passover during which I noticed that on one page in the *Haggadah* (the book of prescribed prayers and rituals) it said in English, "May next year be a year of peace and prosperity," whereas on the facing page in Hebrew it read, "Next year may Messiah, the son of David, come." Those who could still read the Hebrew had their choice of the older or the newer meaning. Those who knew only English had the smooth, modern meaning, without any tension.

Much liberal Judaism in America and elsewhere has developed along similar lines. Liberal Judaism has often contented itself with the affirmation of universal values, seeing biblical and Jewish history as the mere occasion for the manifestation of those values. It has tended to substitute for the biblical covenant "ethical humanism" and for the prophetic demand in the specific historical situation the "progressive revelation" of ideal moral values to be realized in some future "Messianic age." Although I do not hold with those Christians who claim that Unitarians and Universalists are not really Christians and still less with those "born again" Christians who reserve for themselves alone the title of Christian, I suspect that something similar has happened in liberal Christianity.

Our problem is in no way confined to liberalism versus traditionalism. I once read a book on Conservative Judaism that criticized the Orthodox as clinging too much to the past and the Reform as giving in too easily to the present. Actually each of these interpretations of Judaism claims to be what the author held for Conservative Judaism: the *right* tension between past and present, tradition and modernity. And the same is true with all the varied interpretations and reinterpretations of Christianity, Islam, Hinduism, and Buddhism, to name a few.

I do not criticize Fromm and Jung because they cannot accept traditional religion as they understand it, and I respect Kaplan's honesty in trying to accomplish consciously those reevaluations that he feels will be made unconsciously anyway. What I am asking is that we hold the tension, that we not make the problem easier for ourselves than it is. If we do, our traditions will die while our modernity will soon cease to be modern, as is already evident in Kaplan's philosophy of religion.

How many of the American followers of the "universal" teaching of Bahai really understand the origin of Bahai as an Islamic religious and political sect and hold the tension with it? How many practitioners of Transcendental Meditation take seriously the Hindu teaching that is implicit, though regularly denied, in their mantras and meditations? How many of the beat and hippie Zen following in the Fifties and Sixties took seriously the roots of Zen in Buddhism? For that matter, how many Catholics face squarely the anachronism that is involved in the authority of the Pope being based on Jesus' saying, "On this rock [*Petra* Peter] I found my church," when no church even remotely resembling the vast hierarchical structure of the Catholic Church existed in the time of Jesus?

An Orthodox Jewish friend and scholar criticized my chapter in *Touchstones of Reality* on "Jesus: Image of Man or Image of God?" on the ground that my understanding of Jesus' teachings does not conform to that of orthodox Christianity. In so doing, he was following a religious formalism that I must reject in favor of that dialogue of touchstones that in turn deeply affects our own touchstones of reality. Every person has the right to a personal dialogue with the teachings of Jesus, the Buddha, Ramakrishna, Lao-tzu, Black Elk, or the Third Zen Patriarch. But we must not forget that it *is* a dialogue — that we are bringing our own quite unique ground into tension with the great religious teachers. In so far as I was able, I listened obediently and responded wholeheartedly to what Jesus has to say through the admittedly opaque lenses of the Gospels and of the various translations of those Gospels into English. In so doing I do not claim to be a scholar of the New Testament. But neither am I simply reading into Jesus' teachings my own existentialist philosophy. I am listening and responding, entering into dialogue, and bringing the results of that dialogue into my dialogue with others.

9

Dialectic of Spirit and Form

There were three friends
Discussing life.
One said:
"Can men live together
And know nothing of it?
Work together
And produce nothing?
Can they fly around in space
And forget to exist
World without end?"
The three friends looked at each other
And burst out laughing.
They had no explanation.
Thus they were better friends than before.

Then one friend died.
Confucius
Sent a disciple to help the other two
Chant his obsequies.

The disciple found that one friend
Had composed a song.
While the other played a lute,
They sang:
> "Hey, Sung Hu!
> Where'd you go?
> Hey, Sung Hu!
> Where'd you go?
> You have gone
> Where you really were.
> And we are here —
> Damn it! We are here!"

Then the disciple of Confucius burst in on them and
Exclaimed: "May I inquire where you found this in the
Rubrics for obsequies,
This frivolous carolling in the presence of the departed?"

The two friends looked at each other and laughed:
"Poor fellow," they said, "he doesn't know the new liturgy!"[1]

TO HAVE LAID bare the fine or coarse threads with which the
shadow of modernity has been stitched onto the Peter Pan
of religious tradition has not, of course, solved the problem
of the tension between the two. But it may perhaps warn us
against making our already difficult problem worse through
seeking to manipulate old symbols or fabricate new ones in
order to meet the need of the time. We have pointed to the necessity of combining personal uniqueness, the will to be open,
and holding the tension with tradition in order for there to be a
meaningful dynamic, and we have stressed the need to contend
with the tradition in order to make an honest witness to our own
uniqueness and to the Dialogue with the Absurd that has characterized our lives.

Even if all these warnings and admonitions were heeded, it
would not guarantee any smooth continuity of tradition. Quite
the contrary. If, as Buber says, one cannot fill forms that have
grown empty with a new, timely content in a spirit other than
their own, then we may be faced with a period of waiting in the
darkness in order that we may, as Gabriel Vahanian has put it,
"wait without idols." If the philosopher has destroyed the images
of God that swell up and block the way to God, if the finger
pointing to the moon has been taken for the moon itself and
then has been discarded altogether, then what else is there except
for the religious person to "proceed across the darkness to a new
meeting with the nameless Meeter"? If, as Buber says at the end
of "The Dialogue of Heaven and Earth," we await in whatever
form it comes the new appearance of our cruel and kind Lord,
then we cannot predict, much less prescribe, what that form will
be. In this wilderness night, Buber also says, no way can be
pointed out. All we can do is to wait with ready soul until the

morning dawns and a way becomes visible where no one could have foreseen. If this is so, then we cannot demand for pragmatic reasons that tradition be taken over intact from the past as if there were no problem at all.

It was several times suggested to Buber that he should liberate Hasidism from its "confessional limitations," i.e., its integral relationship to the stream of Judaism in which it arose, and make of it a universal religion of mankind. "To take such a 'universal' path would have been pure arbitrariness on my part," Buber replied. It was not necessary for him to leave his ancestral house in order to speak a word to those outside the Jewish tradition, Buber asserted. He could stand in the doorway and utter a word into the street, and the word that was uttered thus, from one "house of exile" to another, would not go astray. In his Foreword to *For the Sake of Heaven*, Buber states that he has no teaching but only wishes to point to realities such as he had made visible in that Hasidic chronicle-novel and in the *Tales of the Hasidim*. Buber undertook this great lifework not for the sake of renewing Judaism alone but also for that of Western man — in order to point to a meaningful image of human existence in the face of the absence of any in our time. Or put in his own language, he saw this time as one of the "eclipse of God"; he pointed out the human contribution to this eclipse; and he pointed to a way that might help us to make ready for a new historical situation in which the finger of God might again be present and discernible in history.

Our most significant insight into the relation of Buber as a modern interpreter and man of faith to the Hasidic tradition is his reply to Rivka Schatz-Uffenheimer, and by implication to her teacher, Gershom Scholem, concerning the charge that the tapestry with which he has portrayed Hasidic teaching is one-sided, insufficiently historical and objective, and "woven of selective strands." Buber did not see or wish others to see his task as an objective, historical one, any more than he saw it as a merely subjective one. It was, rather, a dialogue — between a scholar and a man of faith, on the one hand, and a rich religious tradition on the other — that he brought to the Western world against its own will, because of the need of the hour.

No one, including Scholem, denies Buber a comprehensive and exact knowledge of all the literature of Hasidism, tales and formal teachings alike. But in this historical hour, Buber did not feel that he had the luxury of presenting this tradition simply as an objective historian and scholar. Precisely because of the degeneration of both forms and spirit in the modern world, he felt it necessary to stress one tradition of Hasidism — that which originated with the Baal Shem and focused on the hallowing of the everyday — over the other — that which originated with his successor the Maggid of Mezritch and focused on the nullification of the worldly and the particular for the sake of spiritualization. He was quite ready in his replies to show why he took up the strands that he did and why he let the others lie. But the assumption of his critics, namely that the only valid task was that of full historical exposition, he could not accept.

Instead, Buber put forward a dialogical approach to religion and human experience and to the history of religion that dared to see the interpreter himself as a "filter" for the needs of faith of modern man!

> Since the time in my preoccupation with this subject when I reached a basic study of the sources, i.e., since about 1910 (the early works were not sufficiently based), I have not aimed at presenting a historically or hermeneutically comprehensive presentation of Hasidism. Already at that time there grew in me the consciousness that my task by its nature was a selective one. But at the same time there grew in me an ever firmer certainty that the principle of selection that ruled here did not originate in a subjective preference. In this respect this task of mine is essentially of the same nature as my work on Judaism in general. I have dealt with that in the life and teaching of Judaism which, according to my insight, is its proper truth and is decisive for its function in the previous and future history of the human spirit. This attitude of mine includes valuation, of course, from its base up; but this valuation is one — on this point no doubt has touched me during the whole time — which has its origin in the immovable central existence of values. Since I have attained to the maturity of this insight, I have not made use of a filter; I became a filter.[2]

For Buber to say that he became a filter by no means implies that he was able to take over all the forms of Hasidism and make them his own. In *Philosophical Interpretations* he begged his readers not to identify his own teachings with his interpretations of Hasidism; for the latter used language that he could not himself responsibly employ. "If I had lived in the days when people fought over the word of God and not its caricature," Buber once said, "I too would have left my father's home and become a Hasid." But he also said, "It would have been an unpermissible masquerade for me, who has such a different relationship to the Jewish law, to have become a Hasid." This does not mean that Buber saw his task as purely an intellectual or an interpretative one. On the contrary, he wrote in 1924:

> Since I began my work on Hasidic literature, I have done this work for the sake of the teaching and the way. But at that time I believed that one might relate to them merely as an observer. Since then I have realized that the teaching is there that one may learn it and the way that one may walk on it. The deeper I realized this, so much the more this work, against which my life measured and ventured itself, became for me question, suffering, and also even consolation.[3]

A number of years ago an American rabbi writing in Mordecai Kaplan's journal *The Reconstructionist* pronounced "the contemporary revival of interest in Hasidism" a romantic idealization oftentimes to the point of extravagance. He blamed this "neo-mystical orientation" on "the influence of Martin Buber's literary work in this field during the past half century," a blame in which I myself must share to some degree because I have translated and edited four of Buber's books on Hasidism. The antidote for this neo-Hasidic sickness, said the author, is: "An examination of the elements of irrationality and fantasy in Hasidic doctrine." Such a reexamination "may have a sobering effect upon those who have been overly influenced by the current romanticist conception of Hasidism." After depicting the ignorant and superstitious intellectual climate in which Hasidism grew and spread, he presented an attack on the nonsensical claims for supernatural powers advanced on behalf of the Baal Shem both by the "Besht" himself and his followers.

One of the sources he listed for his material on the Besht is the stories in Buber's *The Legend of the Baal-Shem,* the first of my own translations of Buber's Hasidic works. Nothing could have been more obvious, one would have thought, than that these legends make no claim to historical accuracy. Yet he takes them as reliable historical documents on which to base his criticism. After all this and much more, he comes out with the remarkable conclusion that, whatever Hasidism may have contributed to the Jewish people of the eighteenth century by way of warmth, enthusiasm, joy, and sense of fellowship, Hasidism is an anachronism in our day. "The deep chasm that separates us intellectually from Hasidism," the radical difference in their universe of discourse and ours, makes any attempt to revive Hasidism "as a religious philosophy and movement for our contemporaries" a "confusion of nostalgia and sentimentalism with the imperatives and requirements of a modern man's faith." If there are among our contemporaries some "whose religious backgrounds and mental framework enable them to believe in and practice the Hasidic way of life," then these are men who may be dwelling physically in twentieth-century America, "but they are living intellectually in 18th century Poland."[3]

The "logic" of this testimony in the name of "rational" modern man amounts to saying that if there are some elements in a religious tradition that appear quite foreign to the contemporary American or European, therefore the movement as a whole has nothing to say to us. By the same logic one would have to dismiss the Bible and most of the other world scriptures and myths as utterly irrelevant for "modern man" because there is ample evidence in them of beliefs concerning the supernatural, the demonic, and the miraculous that "modern man" must consider the products of ignorance and superstition or of an outmoded world view.

Nonetheless, this reexamination helps us clarify the problem of the relation between tradition and modernity and with it the dialectic between spirit and form. That Hasidism, to go back to our specific example, could be revived as a really modern movement is difficult, if not impossible, to imagine, despite the successes of the Lubavitcher Hasidim. That it can be revived as an element in a modern religious philosophy is not only imaginable but undeniably actual in a number of important contemporary philosophies of Judaism, such as those of Martin Buber, Abraham J. Heschel, Mische Maisels, Elie Wiesel, my own, and even, to a lesser extent, Leo Baeck, the great representative of liberal Judaism. In the chapter on "Hasidism and Contemporary Man" in *Touchstones of Reality* I claim that Hasidism potentially has some greater and more direct role to play in the modern Jewish and non-Jewish world than that of an element in the thought of various Jewish philosophies. The Hasidic emphases on community, fervor, and the overcoming of the dualism between spirit and life are all of the greatest possible significance for contemporary religious life.

But I would be less than candid if I did not add that while it is possible to take over some of the forms of Hasidic life, such as the *niggunim* or wordless melodies, the dance called the hora, fervor in prayer, the use of the Hasidic tale, and the sense of living community, it is all but impossible for most persons of modern western consciousness to take over others. Those who can, often carry over the trappings of eighteenth-century Poland in an understandable effort not to see the rich tradition of Hasidism dissolve entirely into the secular life of the modern world. In so doing they impede the living dialectic between spirit and form by confining the spirit within the fixed forms of earlier times.

I have used the illustration of Martin Buber's interpretation of Hasidism because it is a subject that I know enough about that I can make the fine distinctions necessary for an understanding of the subtle dialectic between spirit and form. The same focus can be applied to the interaction of spirit and form within any religious tradition. Take, for example, the reformations that have occurred periodically in all great traditional religions — sometimes within them, like the Brethren of the Common Life in fifteenth-century Europe, and sometimes as a disruption that creates new religions, like the Protestant Reformation of Luther, Calvin, Zwingli, and Knox. The root meaning of *reformation* is, of course, re-formation. The claim of every reformation is that it is necessary to break with traditional forms because, although these forms have developed directly and organically from the original events and impulses that gave rise to the religion, somehow along the way they have lost the unique spirit that lay at the heart of the religion.

The reformer, therefore, is one who creates the new in the name of the old. Luther, for example, went back to the tradition of St. Paul and emphasized justification by faith over justification by works. Yet his re-formation did not literally take over the forms of the Church in Paul's day. Rather it created new forms that were held to carry on the original teachings of Christianity more faithfully than the encrustations of the Catholic Church during Luther's time. The Counter-Reformation, in turn, tried to preserve the intactness of the Church through attacking Protestantism, on the one hand, but also through reforming the Church from within, on the other. Similarly, modern Orthodox Judaism arose not, as it claims, as a direct continuation of the tradition of Rabbinical Judaism but as a conscious response to the challenge of Reform Judaism.

Our Dialogue with the Absurd offers us no guarantee of a smooth continuity of religious tradition or, in an age when both religious forms and religious spirit have fallen into question, any sureness of finding the right dialectic between spirit and form. We can speak in general of the traditions and forms of particular religions. No description of Christianity would be complete without mentioning Easter, Good Friday, Christmas, and the Mass, and no description of Judaism would be complete without mentioning the various holidays and sabbath observances that have characterized religious Jews for millenia. But when it comes to our own task of finding the right tension between religious tradition, our personal uniqueness, and the contradictions and absurdities of the world in which we live, no general description any longer has any meaning. Rather there are a thousand particulars that give form in a life and express its basic attitudes, a thousand ways in which one can *be* Torah rather than merely say it.

We are constantly creating new religious forms as we respond to the spirit and are permeated by it, and we do so in faithful dialogue and tension with the spirit and form of tradition. "To be a spiritual heir, one must be a pioneer," writes Abraham Joshua Heschel. But he also writes, "To be worthy of being a pioneer, one must be a spiritual heir"!

10

The Paradox of Religious Leadership

The Grand Augur, who sacrificed the swine and read omens in the sacrifice, came dressed in his long dark robes, to the pig pen, and spoke to the pigs as follows: "Here is my counsel to you. Do not complain about having to die. Set your objections aside, please. Realize that I shall feed you on choice grain for three months. I myself will have to observe strict discipline for ten days and fast for three. Then I will lay out grass mats and offer your hams and shoulders upon delicately carved platters with great ceremony. What more do you want?"

Then, reflecting, he considered the question from the pigs' point of view: "Of course, I suppose you would prefer to be fed with ordinary coarse feed and be left alone in your pen."

But again, seeing it once more from his own viewpoint, he replied: "No, definitely there is a nobler kind of existence! To live in honor, to receive the best treatment, to ride in a carriage with fine clothes, even though at any moment one may be disgraced and executed, that is the noble, though uncertain, destiny that I have chosen for myself."

So he decided against the pigs' point of view, and adopted his own point of view, both for himself and for the pigs also.

How fortunate those swine, whose existence was thus ennobled by one who was at once an officer of state and a minister of religion.

People think that a Sheikh should show miracles and manifest illumination. The requirement in a teacher, however, is only that he should possess all that the disciple needs.

The teacher and the taught together produce the teaching.

No matter where the truth is in your case, your teacher can help you find it. If he applies only one series of method to everyone, he is not a teacher, let alone yours.

Once upon a time there was a dervish. As he was sitting in contemplation, he noticed that there was a sort of devil near him.

The dervish said: "Why are you sitting there, making no mischief?"

The demon raised his head wearily. "Since the theoreticians and would-be teachers of the Path have appeared in such numbers, there is nothing left for me to do."

The Baal-Shem said:

"We say: 'God of Abraham, God of Isaac, and God of Jacob, and not: 'God of Abraham, Isaac, and Jacob, for Isaac and Jacob did not base their work on the searching and service of Abraham; they themselves searched for the unity of the Maker and his service."[1]

THE RELIGIOUS LEADER is a central concern in any phenomenological study of religion. Approached dialogically, this concern necessarily deepens into the contemplation of a phenomenon that is *by its very nature* problematic and even paradoxical. This phenomenon is not that of the inauthentic religious leaders who through all time have usurped divine authority for very human ends of power, wealth, fame, or repression. It is, rather, that of the authentic religious leader. This latter person genuinely wants to lead his or her charges to greater immediacy in their dialogue with the divine. Yet he or she tends to take the place of that immediacy by his very function as leader. What is more, the followers often foist upon the leader the task of vicariously representing them before God with or without his consent and even to the point of idolatry! Again and again in the history of the world's religions, someone who has come to show others an image of the human, a meaningful way of personal and social existence in dialogue with God, has been transformed by those who come after into an image of God, a human image to be worshiped in place of the imageless God, someone to relieve one of the task of being a lamp unto oneself, as the Buddha put it.

This is particularly evident today when, with the growing interest in Oriental religions and their second-, third-, and fourth-hand derivatives, enthusiasts of all ages are being offered a rich and variegated assortment of gurus to choose among. A recent paperback entitled *The Guru Supermarket* shows someone pushing a shopping basket with a pair of spindly brown legs sticking out from below. When I was in Hawaii four years ago, I was given a book entitled *How to Choose a Guru*, conveniently arranged alphabetically. One might think that young people would be hopelessly confused, if it were not for the fact that there *is* a striking resemblance to a supermarket in which one manages to choose among a great variety of brands, variously packaged and prices, and somehow trusts that one has made the right choice!

The past decades have seen the phenomenon of many young people forsaking their homes *and* their cultures to become members of any number of handy cults. Accusations of brainwashing on the part of confused parents have been equalled by accusations of counter-brainwashing when these parents call in self-styled experts to deprogram their children and try to get them back. The courts are understandably confused about when the absolute allegiance of a young person to this or that religious leader is to be understood as an act of faith and when it is to be understood as the consequence of manipulation! Meanwhile, the alternative religions have become big business, presented with all the media techniques of what used to be called "Madison Avenue," salting away millions in Swiss banks, building up powerful organizations and churches that claim exemption from taxes and public scrutiny. Others come along and present a smoothly packaged, sophisticated, expensive, synthetic amalgam of many of these trends. Such cults and churches train teachers all over the world, raise ever higher the prices of what the leaders impart, and establish international universities and centers of research. They sponsor prestigious conferences on the unity of science and religion replete with Nobel Prize laureates. The seemingly primitive displays of their followers with their robes, drums, and copies of books to be sold at airports and train stations, are matched by ever-slicker magazines and research foundations. Nor are the pentecostal movements in Protestant and Catholic churches today one whit behind with their powerful apparatus of radio and television programs, publications, armies of young workers, students set to monitor their professors' teaching of religion, and arrays of charismatic personalities, to follow whose teachings and dictates is itself counted a religious act!

Because of the complexity of modern society and the sophistication of the media, the problem of religious leadership is greatly aggravated, but it is by no means new. When T. S. Eliot's *Thomas à Becket* identifies his own will with the will of God and sees himself as nothing but a selfless instrument in God's hands, the greatest humility becomes, unconsciously, the greatest arrogance. Thomas's opening speech in Eliot's poem-play *Murder in the Cathedral* already sets the whole of the dramatic action within the framework of an objective heavenly hierarchy in which each of the saints and martyrs has a destined place to which he is called:

> They know and do not know, that action is suffering
> And suffering is action. Neither does the actor suffer
> Nor the patient act. But both are fixed
> In an eternal action, an eternal patience
> To which all must consent that it may be willed
> And which all must suffer that they may will it,
> That the pattern may subsist, for the pattern is the action
> And the suffering, that the wheel may turn and still
> Be forever still.

Thomas's sense of his destined place in this heavenly hierarchy is expressed with utmost clarity in his Christmas Sermon in the Interlude between Part I and Part II. A Christian martyr is no accident, he says, and still less is it "the effect of a man's will to become a Saint."

> A martyr, a saint, is always made by the design of God, for His love to men, to warn them and to lead them, to bring them back to His ways. A martyrdom is never the design of man; for the true martyr is he who has become the instrument of God, who has lost his will in the will of God, not lost it but found it, for he has found freedom in submission to God. The martyr no longer desires anything for himself, not even the glory of martyrdom.... So in Heaven

the Saints are most high, having made themselves most low.

Thomas's statement that the martyr does not even desire the glory of martyrdom is unconvincing in Thomas's case because the sermon is centered around Thomas's own expectation of becoming a martyr: "I do not think I shall ever preach to you again; ... it is possible that in a short time you may have yet another martyr." Four days later Thomas insists, against the protests of the priests, that the knights who have come to kill him be admitted to the cathedral. In so doing, he puts his action once again within a heavenly framework and one, moreover, that neither priests nor knights nor any common man can understand:

> It is not in time that my death shall be known;
> It is out of time that my decision is taken
> If you call that decision
> To which my whole being gives entire consent.
> I give my life
> To the Law of God above the Law of Man.
> Those who do not the same
> How should they know what I do?
> How should you know what I do? ...

Thomas's pride and his sense of superiority to all the other actors in this drama is as clear in these final speeches as it was at the beginning.

The inescapable corollary of this view is that the common man is someone who must blindly follow the charismatic leader and thank God at the same time for bestowing such undeserved grace on the totally unworthy, all of which is expressed again and again by the chorus of the women of Canterbury. Their final chorus, the last lines of the play itself, is an acknowledgment by them of their essential, almost natural inferiority to the saints and martyrs through whom they find salvation:

> Forgive us, O Lord, we acknowledge ourselves as type of
>   the common man,
> Of the men and women who shut the door and sit by the fire;

Who fear the blessing of God, the loneliness of the night of
  God, the surrender required, the deprivation inflicted;
Who fear the injustice of men less than the justice of God;
Who fear the hand at the window, the fire in the thatch,
  the fist in the tavern, the push into the canal,
Less than we fear the love of God.
We acknowledge our trespass, our weakness, our fault; we
  acknowledge
That the sin of the world is upon our heads; that the blood
  of the martyrs and the agony of the saints
Is upon our heads....
Blessed Thomas, pray for us.[2]

The prototype of this hierarchical view of religious leadership
is not to be found in the teachings of Jesus or even of St. Paul
but in the *Republic* of Plato, the fountainhead of Greek and all
of western philosophy. Deeply embittered by the martyrdom
that the Athenian democracy forced upon his teacher Socrates,
Plato envisaged a prototype of the authoritarian state in which
the various castes are governed by the royal myth, or lie, and in
which the Philosopher-King, the highest representative of the
Guardian Class, does not just know the Good but is seen as identical with it!

Yet the problematic phenomenon of religious leadership is
found no less in the biblical tradition, which fused with the
Greek in creating traditional Christianity. We need only think of
the profound irony in the speech attributed to the Lord in which
he tells the reluctant prophet Samuel to go ahead and crown
Saul king as the people demand:

> But the thing displeased Samuel when they said, "Give us
> a king to govern us." And Samuel prayed to the Lord. And
> the Lord said to Samuel, "Hearken to the voice of the peo-
> ple in all that they say to you; for they have not rejected
> you, but they have rejected me from being king over them.
> According to all the deeds which they have done to me,
> from the day I brought them up out of Egypt even to this
> day, forsaking me and serving other gods, so they are also
> doing to you. Now then, hearken to their voice; only, you
> shall solemnly warn them, and show them the ways of the
> king who shall reign over them."

So Samuel told all the words of the Lord to the people who were asking a king from him. He said, "These will be the ways of the king who will reign over you: he will take your sons and appoint them to his chariots and to be his horsemen, and to run before his chariots; and he will appoint for himself commanders of thousands and commanders of fifties, and some to plow his ground and to reap his harvest, and to make his implements of war and the equipment of his chariots. He will take your daughters to be perfumers and cooks and bakers. He will take the best of your fields and vineyards and olive orchards and give them to his servants. He will take the tenth of your grain and of your vineyards and give it to his officers and to his servants. He will take your menservants and maidservants, and the best of your cattle and your asses, and put them to his work. He will take the tenth of your flocks, and you shall be his slaves. And in that day you will cry out because of your king, whom you have chosen for yourselves; but the Lord will not answer you in that day."

—RSV, 1 Samuel 8:4-18

The relevance of this passage to the problematic of religious leadership does not arise simply from the fact that Samuel is the prophet and judge who rules the people in the name of God and who anoints Saul king in God's name. It also arises from the fact that the king too is seen as a religious leader, one whose task it is to continue the Covenant, to make real the kingship of God in every aspect of community life. It is out of the failure of the kings in this task that the Hebrew prophets arise, bringing to the king the demand of the covenant, saying like Amos to the priest at Beth-El, "I am no prophet, nor son of a prophet.... But when the lion roars, who can but tremble? When the Lord God speaks, who can but prophesy?" And it is out of the repeated failure of the prophets that the Messianic vision of the *true* king arises in the Immanuel of Isaiah and the "suffering servant of the Lord" of Deutero-Isaiah. The word *Messiah*, indeed, is nothing other than an Anglicization of the Hebrew *Meschiach*, which means "anointed." Yet with what profound irony and misgiving is the first king of Israel anointed by Samuel!

In a penetrating essay, "Biblical Leadership," Buber points out that before the advent of the kings it is the weak and the humble, rather than the strong, who are chosen to lead, and that they carry out their leadership not through historical success and power but through failure. "The Bible knows nothing of this intrinsic value of success." The failures of both Moses and David are given in detail, and "this glorification of failure culminates in the long line of prophets whose existence is failure through and through." The *servant of the Lord*, likewise, is one who sees his strength and readiness as all in vain. His mouth is like a sharp sword, but the Lord has hid him in the shadow of his hand. God has made him into a polished shaft, an arrow that is ready to fly, and then has concealed him in his quiver (Isaiah 49:2). Yet this failure does not mean that the biblical leader does no work. His work is done not in the heights of power but in the depths of history; his truth is hidden in obscurity.

> This existence in the shadow, in the quiver, is the final word of the leaders in the biblical world, this enclosure in failure, in obscurity, even when one stands in the blaze of public life, in the presence of the whole national life.[3]

What Buber writes here can only be understood within the context of a dialogical approach not only to religion but to history. Within this context the problematic of religious leadership deepens into a paradox. Biblical history, Buber suggests, is the history of God's disappointments in the dialogue with the people who continually fail to answer and continually rise up and try to answer. The way of this history leads from disappointment to disappointment and beyond them to the messianic. Biblical leadership, correspondingly, falls into five types according to the great stages in the history of the people. First, there is that of the Patriarchs — Abraham, Isaac, and Jacob — who beget the people. Second, there is that of the Leader — Moses — who leads the people in their wandering. Third, there is that of the Judges, who rise up on special occasions to set the people right, who refuse, like Gideon, to be crowned king because God alone is King, and who repeatedly fail in their task of establishing a direct kingship of God. Fourth, there is that of the Kings, who are anointed to make real the kingship of God and on whom the

Bible lays the blame for the failure in the dialogue with God. Fifth, there is that of the Prophets, who call King and people to account for their failure in the dialogue, who cut themselves off from the natural instincts that bind them to community, and whose reward is to be treated by the people as their enemy. All these types of religious leadership lead to the idea of the messianic leader through whom at last an answer will be spoken with man's whole being that will answer the word of God, an answer that is, thus, an earthly consummation in and with mankind.

> This is what the messianic belief means, the belief in the real leader, in the setting right of the dialogue, in God's disappointment being at an end. And when a fragment of an apocryphal gospel has God say to Jesus: "In all the prophets have I awaited thee, that thou wouldst come and I rest in thee, for thou art My rest," this is the late elaboration of a truly Jewish conception.[4]

In the chapter, "Jesus: Image of Man or Image of God?" in *Touchstones of Reality*, I ask, in fact, whether Jesus does not stand in this messianic succession. When Jesus asks his disciples, "What do men say that I am? And what do you think that I am?" is he asking a real question as someone with a unique place in the messianic history of Judaism that cannot be understood by any already existing category? Or is he speaking out of the sure knowledge of his divinity, the Messiah Come, or even, as in Byzantine times, the Pantocrator?

The history of the great religions is bound up, Buber suggests, with the problem: How do human beings stand the test of anointing? This is not a test of them as individuals in isolation but precisely as leaders looked to by the people, often looked to for success or at the very least to take the place of the people in the dialogue with God. The history of the kings is the history of the failure of the anointed to realize the promise of his anointing, and the rise of messianism correspondingly is the belief in the anointed king who realizes the promise of his anointing.

But the significance of the biblical leader is not limited to the context of the biblical Covenant and biblical messianism. "The biblical leaders are the foreshadowings of the dialogical man, of the man who commits his whole being to God's dialogue with the world, and who stands firm throughout this dialogue." These are men who are leaders precisely insofar as they allow themselves to be led, "insofar as they take upon themselves the responsibility for that which is entrusted to them," and make it real. What we are accustomed to call history is from the biblical standpoint only the great failure, the refusal to enter into the dialogue, not the failure in the dialogue, as exemplified by the biblical leader. By the same token, the significance of the failure of the latter is not limited to the history of biblical messianism but casts light on the paradox of religious leadership in general:

> The way, the real way, from the Creation to the Kingdom is trod not on the surface of success, but in the deep of failure. The real work, from the biblical point of view, is the late-recorded, the unrecorded, the anonymous work. The real work is done in the shadow, in the quiver. Official leadership fails more and more, leadership devolves more and more upon the secret.[5]

What is in question here is not the familiar contrast between the personal charisma of Francis of Assisi and official charisma — "the divinity that doth hedge round the head of a king," that atrocious caricature of biblical leadership that the monarchs of France arrogated to themselves by "the divine right of kings." It is rather the contrast between the genuine charismatic leader like Theodor Herzl, who identified himself so totally with the cause of the Zionist movement that he founded that questioning him was, to him, tantamount to disloyalty to the cause, and those persons like Martin Buber and his friends in the "Democratic Fraction" who represented, if anything, only the "negative charisma" of the unsuccessful. In his autobiographical fragment, "The Cause and the Person," Buber asks whether there might not be yet another reality, different from that of obvious world history:

> ... a reality hidden and powerless because it has not come into power; whether there might not be, therefore, men with a mission who have not been called to power and yet are, in essence, men who have been summoned; whether

excessive significance has not perhaps been ascribed to the circumstances that separate the one class of men from the other; whether success is the only criterion; whether the unsuccessful man is not destined at times to gain a belated, perhaps posthumous, perhaps even anonymous victory which even history refuses to record; whether, indeed, when even this does not happen, a blessing is not spoken, nonetheless, to these abandoned ones, a word that confirms them; whether there does not exist a "dark" charisma.[6]

The history of Hasidism is an especially poignant exemplification of the contrast between these two types of leadership. Originally, to be sure, the Baal Shem and those who followed him were recognized leaders of the community who saw it as their task to bring their followers into greater immediacy in the dialogue with God. After several generations, however, dynasties of zaddikim developed in which it was no longer personal spiritual qualities but, like the Kings of the Bible, the succession of birth that determined on whom the leadership of the communities of the Hasidim would devolve. The zaddik, or rebbe, was not just a priest with a priestly function, but a leader responsible for the total life of his community and of each family and each individual in it. Therefore, his power for healing and help could equally easily become a power for domination and exploitation.

Some zaddikim had sufficient wholeness that they could descend into the whirlpool and help the afflicted and troubled souls without getting stuck themselves. Others found themselves sucked down into the whirlpool. Still others were like the "wicked," of whom the Seer of Lublin spoke, who did not turn even on the threshold of hell; "for they thought they were being sent to hell to redeem the souls of others"! And some dark and enigmatic figures like Menahem Mendel of Kotzk abjured the task of leadership in the last years of their lives and compared themselves to the "Sacred Goat." Originally the Sacred Goat walked up and down on the earth and the tips of his black horns touched the stars. But then he gave of his horns to countless suffering and demanding persons. Now he still walks up and down on the earth, but he no longer has horns with which to touch the stars!

Buber's great Hasidic chronicle-novel *For the Sake of Heaven*
is a profound study of the paradox of religious leadership within
Hasidism but also, by implication, in the modern world where a
false messianic on every side leads people to seek the goal of justice by the ways of injustice. This novel is based on the tragic tension between two actual historical figures — the Seer of Lublin and
his disciple, the Yehudi, or "the Holy Jew." The Seer of Lublin
wishes to hasten the coming of redemption through magical, mystical intentions and prayers that will strengthen Napoleon, whom
he identifies with the apocryphal Gog of the land of Magog, and
thus force God to send the Messiah. The holy Yehudi, in contrast,
stays clear of magic and teaches that redemption can come only
through our turning back to God with the whole of our individual and communal existence. The Seer's religious leadership rests,
correspondingly, on that "miracle, mystery, and authority" that
Dostoevsky's Grand Inquisitor espoused, whereas the Yehudi's
rests on the call to the turning that respects the power of response of every individual person.

At the Seer's suggestion, the Yehudi leaves him and founds a
congregation of his own, even while remaining a loyal disciple of
the Seer. Through the Seer's emphasis on the divine power of the
zaddik and through the awe of his disciples, the Seer holds the
place of an oriental potentate in his congregation. The Yehudi, in
contrast, preserves an informal and democratic relation with his
disciples. The Seer uses his disciples for magic purposes; the
Yehudi helps his disciples find the path they seek to pursue of
and for themselves. He teaches his disciples that man's turning is
not for the sake of individual salvation alone but for the redemption of the whole of creation — for the sake of the Shekinah,
God's indwelling glory, which is in exile. Redemption takes place
not in isolation, moreover, but in a communal life of justice,
love, and consecration.[7]

The death of the Yehudi, who deliberately enters into a fatal
ecstasy in order to bring back a message from Heaven for the
Seer, shares with Jesus the paradigm of the suffering servant. The
moments before his death are given up entirely to the thought of
the Shekinah, for whom he has suffered and endeavored during
his life. Repeating the words of Deutero-Isaiah about the servant

of the Lord, the lamb who is led to slaughter, the Yehudi dies with the phrase on his lips, "The only one to declare Thy oneness." Of all the religious leaders who work "for the sake of heaven" in this novel, only the Yehudi has refused to work for redemption with external means or to accept a division of the world between God and the devil or a redemption that is anything less than the redemption of all evil. His struggle with the Seer is a part of this affirmation of the oneness of God. It prevents us from seeing the conflict of the story as one between good and evil. Rather it is, like the conflict between Herzl and Buber, a tragedy in that special sense in which Buber defines it, the "cruel antitheticalness" of existence itself, the fact that each is as he or she is and there are not sufficient resources in the relationship to bring the opposition into genuine dialogue and to prevent it from crystallizing into oppositeness.

The Yehudi is a charismatic figure, like Thomas à Becket, he, too, is the center of a religious community. But he is not so through appointment, like Thomas, but because he is the person that he is. His charisma is personal and not official. Thomas stands closer to the Seer, who receives a special reverence and credence from his disciples and stands at the head of a structured, authoritarian community. From the Seer's point of view the Yehudi's martyrdom might resemble that of Thomas à Becket, because the Seer hopes that it will help in his magical-apocalyptic actions to bring about the coming of the Messiah. But from the point of view of the Yehudi, his dying is not part of any predestined design or any spiritual hierarchy, and he accomplishes no purpose by his death in the sense of a means that can lead to some end. He is simply an image of a human being who takes suffering on himself. He stands, Buber suggests, in the succession of figures who, in every generation, become Deutero-Isaiah's "suffering servant of the Lord." But he is also and equally the image of a person who refuses to allow the tragic contradiction of existence to cut him off from faithful relationship with the teacher whom he acknowledges even while he opposes him. The Yehudi does not speak of his enemies as beasts and madmen, as does Eliot's Thomas. "You are not to think that those who persecute me do so out of an evil heart," he says to a disciple. "The fundamental motive of their persecution of me is to serve Heaven." He does not leave the evil of the world unredeemed; he brings the tragic contradiction into his relationship with God.[8]

In Western Europe and America, the traditional *rav* of Eastern Europe and the *zaddik*, or rebbe, of Hasidism, was succeeded by the "rabbi," who is supposed to combine the functions of both — be teacher, interpreter of the law, spiritual inspirer, and counsellor to the troubled and the needy. Sometimes this leads to being all things to all people and very little to any, which is also true of the Protestant minister and the Catholic priest. When I was Visiting Professor at Hebrew Union College in Cincinnati in 1956, I came to know one of the first-year students, an exceptionally fine man who at the age of 45 had given up a thriving music business in Honolulu to undertake five years of arduous training which would lead to his becoming a Reform rabbi at the age of 50! One night when he and I were having peanut butter sandwiches in the kitchen, he asked me, "Doctor, how is it you never thought of becoming a rabbi?" "I have enough difficulty maintaining my integrity as a teacher," I replied.

I did not mean by this that either teachers or rabbis are persons without integrity. What I meant was that the greater the demand placed upon one by one's students or one's congregants, the more difficult it is to maintain one's integrity — to hold in authentic tension one's uniqueness as a person and one's function in one's social role and to reject the pseudo-confirmation that comes from being elevated above the people. It goes without saying that the religious leader is in far greater danger, in this regard, than the teacher, who is (occasionally) respected in this society but hardly venerated and certainly not asked to be a spiritual stand-in for the student. Nor was I thinking of my questioner when I replied, but of his fellow seminarians, mostly far younger men who were being taught to intone and do casework but had not had the time to work through to a personal religious position of their own or to personal maturity. When these young men became rabbis, they would be turned into "father figures" and "spiritual guides" by their congregants!

Just how central this problem is today, even among the most

traditional of religions, is shown by the controversies surrounding whether priests must be celibate and cannot marry, whether women can become rabbis, ministers, and priests, whether avowed homosexuals may properly serve as religious leaders. These issues would not be nearly so bitterly fought if it were not for the investment that parishioners have in their religious leaders being fathers, guides, moral exemplars, and spiritual substitutes for them.

The *paradox* of religious leadership is only plumbed if we recognize that in a dialogical approach to religion the ultimate touchstone is the immediacy of contact with ultimate reality, whether that contact be made in prayer, cult, creed, or the countless concrete happenings of the everyday. We must recognize equally that all religious tradition is carried on by a dialectic between immediacy and mediacy, directness and indirectness, dialogue and intellectual dialectic, spirit and form. God, according to Hasidic teaching, is like a father who brings himself to the level of the child in order progressively to lead him upward until he can stand on his own feet as an equal. The same, but much more so, could be said of the religious leader, an excellent example of which is the Zen master Bankei:

> When Bankei held his seclusion-weeks of meditation, pupils from many parts of Japan came to attend. During one of these gatherings a pupil was caught stealing. The matter was reported to Bankei with the request that the culprit be expelled. Bankei ignored the case.
>
> Later the pupil was caught in a similar act, and again Bankei disregarded the matter. This angered the other pupils, who drew up a petition asking for the dismissal of the thief, stating that otherwise they would leave in a body.
>
> When Bankei had read the petition he called everyone before him. "You are wise brothers," he told them. "You know what is right and what is not right. You may go somewhere else to study if you wish, but this poor brother does not even know right from wrong. Who will teach him if I do not? I am going to keep him here even if all the rest of you leave."
>
> A torrent of tears cleansed the face of the brother who had stolen. All desire to steal had vanished.[9]

How can the religious leader stand the test of "anointing," i.e., of the responsibility of religious leadership if his or her followers desire to find security in him or her, long for a symbiotic union in which they are dominated by him or her, or even magically desire to possess what the other one has and they feel they lack? Idolatry is not just a matter of wooden idols, or of silver and gold ones, but of giving up responsibility for oneself to another.

One sabbath Rabbi Zevi Hirsh interrupted his teachings at the third meal and said:
"There are hasidim who travel to their rabbi and say that save for him there is no rabbi in all the world. That is idol worship. What should they say? They should say: 'Every rabbi is good for his people, but our rabbi is best for what concerns us.'"[10]

Imitation can also be a form of idolatry:

The gatekeeper in the capital city of Sung became such an expert mourner after his father's death, and so emaciated himself with fasts and austerities, that he was promoted to high rank in order that he might serve as a model of ritual observance.
As a result of this, his imitators so deprived themselves that half of them died. The others were not promoted.[11]

Just as children need parents and pupils teachers, so we need religious leaders. Yet we need ones who do not put themselves in the place of God, ones who know, as Lao-tzu enjoined, how to stay in the front of people without their knowing. By this latter I do not mean facilitators, who reject the name of teacher but are often more authoritarian than any teacher. I mean rather those who understand in their very beings the difference between *imposing upon others* through eloquent sermons, superior mediamanship, manipulation, and propaganda, and *helping others to unfold*, each in his or her own way and according to his or her unique relation to the truth.

On the eve of the New Year Rabbi Mendel entered the House of Prayer. He surveyed the many people who had come together from near and far. "A fine crowd!" he called out to them. "But I want you to know that I cannot carry you all on my shoulders. Every one of you must work for himself."

In modern times a great deal of nonsense is talked about masters and disciples, and about the inheritance of a master's teaching by favorite pupils, entitling them to pass the truth on to their adherents. Of course Zen should be imparted in this way, from heart to heart, and in the past it was really accomplished. Silence and humility reigned rather than profession and assertion. The one who received such a teaching kept the matter hidden even after twenty years. Not until another discovered through his own need that a real master was at hand was it learned that the teaching had been imparted, and even then the occasion arose quite naturally and the teaching made its way in its own right. Under no circumstance did the teacher even claim "I am the successor of So-and-so." Such a claim would prove quite the contrary.

The Zen master Mu-nan had only one successor. His name was Shoju. After Shoju had completed his study of Zen, Mu-nan called him into his room. "I am getting old," he said, "and as far as I know, Shoju, you are the only one who will carry on this teaching. Here is a book. It has been passed down from master to master for seven generations. I also have added many points according to my understanding. The book is very valuable, and I am giving it to you to represent your successorship."

"If the book is such an important thing, you had better keep it," Shoju replied. "I received your Zen without writing and am satisfied with it as it is."

"I know that," said Mu-nan. "Even so, this work has been carried from master to master for seven generations, so you may keep it as a symbol of having received the teaching. Here."

The two happened to be talking before a brazier. The instant Shoju felt the book in his hands he thrust it into the flaming coals. He had no lust for possessions.

Mu-nan, who never had been angry before, yelled: "What are you doing!"

Shoju shouted back: "What are you saying!"[12]

In the end what is decisive in religious leadership is not *expounding* the Torah but *being* the Torah, not performing miracles but the way in which one lives one's daily life.

When Bankei was preaching at Ryumon temple, a Shinshu priest, who believed in salvation through the repetition of the name of the Buddha of Love, was jealous of his large audience and wanted to debate with him.

Bankei was in the midst of a talk when the priest appeared, but the fellow made such a disturbance that Bankei stopped his discourse and asked about the noise.

"The founder of our sect," boasted the priest, "had such miraculous powers that he held a brush in his hand on one bank of the river, his attendant held up a paper on the other bank, and the teacher wrote the holy name of Amida through the air. Can you do such a wonderful thing?"

Bankei replied lightly: "Perhaps your fox can perform that trick, but that is not the manner of Zen. My miracle is that when I feel hungry I eat, and when I feel thirsty I drink."[13]

This distinction also applies to those who impose their views in good faith because they sincerely believe the word they speak is not their own but God's. A young graduate student at the Humanistic Psychology Institute at Sonoma State College accused me of tearing the covers off the Bible, of starting with the Buddha rather than with where the Bible starts, with Jesus Christ. Asked by one of his fellow students, "What would you feel if we said, 'That is your bag and this is ours'?" he replied, "Your bag is false because you speak with the pride of men. But mine is true because I speak with the words of God."

What gives us enough ground to stand on so that we can find our own uniqueness, our inmost passion which stirs and calls most deeply our heart, and yet be open to others? "This is *my* way, what is yours?" says Nietzsche's Zarathustra when asked about *the* way, and adds: "As for *the* way it does not exist." For me, the ultimate test of religious leadership is twofold: First, does it help those who are led to find their own ground rather than coasting along forever in dependence upon guru, zaddik, minister, or priest? Second, does it lead to greater openness to dialogue with the world, toward building a "community of otherness," or does it lead to ever greater closedness in which one takes refuge in the cult or church of the like-minded, the community of affinity? These two questions necessarily belong together, for the heart of the community of otherness lies in the dialogue of touchstones among the members of the community. In this dialogue the religious leader needs his or her followers as much as the followers need the leader if religious reality is to arise between them.

It is told:

> Once, on the evening after the Day of Atonement, the moon was hidden behind the clouds and the Baal Shem could not go out to say the Blessing of the New Moon. This weighed heavily on his spirit, for now, as often before, he felt that destiny too great to be gauged depended on the work of his lips. In vain he concentrated his intrinsic power on the light of the wandering star, to help it throw off the heavy sheath: whenever he sent some one out, he was told that the clouds had grown even more lowering. Finally he gave up hope.
>
> In the meantime, the hasidim who knew nothing of the Baal Shem's grief, had gathered in the front room of the house and begun to dance, for on this evening that was their way of celebrating with festal joy the atonement for the year, brought about by the zaddik's priestly service. When their holy delight mounted higher and higher, they invaded the Baal Shem's chamber, still dancing. Overwhelmed by their own frenzy of happiness they took him by the hands, as he sat there sunk in gloom, and drew him into the round. At this moment, someone called outside. The night had suddenly grown light; in greater radiance than ever before, the moon curved on a flawless sky.[14]

In raising these questions, we have already anticipated the two-directional answer to the query of our final chapter, "Is Religion the Enemy of Mankind?"

Part five

Religion and
Human Wholeness

11

Spontaneity, Decision, and Personal Wholeness

> In the age when life on earth was full, no one paid any special attention to worthy men, nor did they single out the man of ability. Rulers were simply the highest branches on the tree, and the people were like deer in the woods. They were honest and righteous without realizing that they were "doing their duty." They loved each other and did not know that this was "love of neighbor." They deceived no one yet they did not know that they were "men to be trusted." They were reliable and did not know that this was "good faith." They lived freely together giving and taking, and did not know that they were generous. For this reason their deeds have not been narrated. They made no history.
>
> Rabbi Yudel, a man known for his fear of God and the harsh penances he imposed on himself, once came to visit the maggid of Zlotchov. Rabbi Mikhal said to him: "Yudel, you are wearing a hair shirt against your flesh. If you were not given to sudden anger, you would not need it, and since you are given to sudden anger, it will not help you."
>
> The Seer of Lublin said: "I prefer a passionate opponent to a lukewarm adherent. For the passionate opponent might still turn to you with all of his passion. But from a lukewarm adherent there is nothing more to be hoped."[1]

I F RELIGION were pure dialogue and pure immediacy, there would be no need for a philosophy of religion, but neither would there be any such thing as religious forms and structures, traditions, and organizations. Actually religion is made up of a complex interaction between immediacy and form, flowing and structure, and the real issues are not the choice between the one side and the other but the nature of the blend, which often adds up to the emphasis that is needed at any given historical juncture. Lao-tzu's respect for spontaneity and Confucius's respect for propriety both have their place in an understanding approach to religion, whatever its nature and manifestation. Thus an adequate philosophy of religion must be concerned with both dialogue and dialectic, meaning by the latter the swinging interaction between the immediacy of dialogue and the mediacy of structure and form.

This dialectic must be understood on many different levels. It takes place even within the individual person who cannot persist in immediacy of dialogue and who uses touchstones of reality, insights, symbols, and concepts both as residues of earlier moments of dialogue and helpers to enter into new dialogue. For the master and disciple, the brotherhood, the tribe, the church, synagogue, denomination, and sect, this dialectic is multifaceted and multileveled. What is more, the concern for continuance — for the preservation and perseverance of the religious tradition — regularly makes the emphasis upon form and structure so great that the dialectic itself is endangered, and what is passed down is a set of structures and forms which no longer move back to that immediacy which gave rise to them.

A dynamic, as opposed to a static and merely descriptive, approach must seek to plumb some of the problems to which this swinging interaction and the encrustations which prevent it give rise. To examine them all would be an encyclopedic task. What we can do is to try to fathom some representative problems from the side of the religious person, on the one hand, and some from the side of the religious tradition, on the other.

The problem for the religious person is not unlike that of the alternation between the I-Thou and the I-It in general. Our passion needs direction; our excitement needs containment; our moments of ecstasy must alternate with moments of simple calm. The right rhythm of alternation between one and the other differs from person to person and situation to situation. Therefore, it cannot be specified by any technique but only apprehended by moment-by-moment awareness, "a heart of wisdom." Both within tradition itself and in any given living generation, there are books and persons that act as purveyors of wisdom. Yet few are the religious persons fortunate enough to have gurus, rebbes, priests, or roshis sufficiently attuned to their uniqueness that they can give them what they need at that moment. That is why the Seer of Lublin said: "It is impossible to tell men what way they should take. For one way to serve God is through the teachings, another through prayer, another through fasting, and still another through eating." Although he himself was a *zaddik*, a Hasidic rebbe, in this saying, at least, he referred his disciples not to the superior wisdom of the *zaddik* but to that of their own heart: "Everyone should carefully observe what way his heart draws him to, and then choose this way with all his strength."

Unfortunately, many substitute social awareness for the awareness of their central-most wish — that calling and drawing of the heart which, if anything, gives us our profoundest glimpse into the meaning of the "I." But even where one does not turn away to the oldest tradition or the latest fad for guidance, the heart itself often seems to offer promptings that are confused and contradictory. Whether one holds with Genesis 6 and 8 that it is only the *imaginings* of man's heart, and not the heart itself, that are evil from youth onward or with Jeremiah, "The heart is deceitful and infinitely corrupt. Who can understand it?" or follows the Zen text on "Trusting in the Heart," it is clear that the subjective world to which we refer ourselves is not seldom as perplexing and misleading as the objective. One answer to this perplexity is implicit in the Seer's statement, namely, the distinction between the many impulses that throng and crowd one another, each calling for attention and gratification, and the powerful innermost wish that calls the heart itself.

What we mean by the *heart* is the wholeness of the person, and here too one can be mistaken. Human history is littered with sad exemplars of mistaking intensity, logic, emotion, or inspiration for human wholeness. One of the reasons such a mistake is made is that we tend to trust one of our faculties more than another and wish to identify the *I* with that faculty preeminently. For many persons, this expresses itself as a trust in reason as objective and a mistrust of emotions or feelings as subjective. In our day, on the other hand, some correctives to this tendency have swung us so far in the other direction that intuitions and feelings are given our sole confidence, and reason and logic are depreciated and looked down upon. The contemporary emphasis upon feeling leads many today to confuse the reciprocal release of pent-up emotions and deeply repressed feelings with genuine relationship, as if real mutuality must automatically emerge from self-expression. It is understandable that many people who are intellectually detached or in some other way cut off from their emotions hope to break through their blocks and get back to what they really feel. Unfortunately, many such people are as cut off from the feelings of others as their own, in addition to which they are programmed to listen for cues and to put other people on pegs rather than to really hear them. This situation is made still worse when they fall into labeling, identifying feeling with reality and declaring that *their* words are really feelings while the words of others are intellectual abstractions, or "merely words."

Our feelings are important, of course. We must go back to them and start there. But there are many people today who seem to want to end there, and in so doing they miss the path to human wholeness. When we have a deep and perhaps violent emotional breakthrough, it is a revelation of something hidden in the depths of our souls, something heretofore perhaps entirely unsuspected. If this emotion that has been brought to the light is intense and if it is associated with religious symbols or cults, we can easily be misled into seeing it as the only reality and into depreciating what before was accessible to the conscious mind. An equal and corollary danger to our wholeness as persons is to see the breakthrough as complete in itself, instead of seeing it as a little light lighting up a long, dark road up a mountain and down into a canyon — a road that we have to walk in our everyday life before this breakthrough can be made lasting and meaningful.

The concentration on feeling most often means the concentration on individual feeling, the feelings experienced within us and expressed to others. This dualism between inner feeling and outer facade may lead us to overlook the social matrix and the social nature of feelings, especially as they are connected with religious symbols and with cultic activities, such as praying, communion, and individual or group worship. The temper of the religious tradition and the religious group and the emphases of the religious leader inevitably affect our attitude toward our own emotions so that what we express is not the raw emotion but the emotion shaped by our attitude as a member of this religious group. This is nowhere more strongly demonstrated, perhaps, than in a revival meeting or in the pentecostal phenomenon of speaking in tongues. The social matrix of feeling is seldom recognized. Instead, feeling is sometimes regarded as a substantive reality that is in us and only needs to be brought out.

We cannot avoid the route of feeling, yet expecting and demanding feeling can get in the way of true spontaneity and may lead, instead, to that supreme contradiction in terms — *planned spontaneity*. It takes a great deal of listening to allow what happens to come forth spontaneously — not inhibited by an image of oneself that tells one in advance what one's strengths and weaknesses are supposed to be, but also not inhibited by the group pressure to express the emotions approved of, expected, and even demanded by the group. We would like to live more intensely, more vitally, more fully. We would like to share love and joy. Often in religious groups this is exactly what happens. But the more we aim at this goal, the more one part of us will be looking on from the sidelines, anticipating and measuring results, and for that very reason not living fully in the present, not being whole.

The same applies to our concern with our own sinfulness and our desire for repentance. "Rake the muck this way, rake the muck that way, it is still muck," said the Rabbi of Ger. "What does Heaven get out of it? While I am brooding over my sins, I could be stringing pearls for the delight of Heaven!" Our problem is that we are divided within ourselves, that we are not in genuine dialogue with one another, and that we live immersed in a deep existential mistrust. These sicknesses of our human condition cannot be overcome simply by the will to wholeness, openness, and trust or by the magic of technique.

In the years since the mystical experiences of which I tell in *Touchstones of Reality*, I have again and again been troubled by the question of how I can put together the overwhelming intensity and certainty of those experiences and the shattering of security which followed. In a long letter I wrote in November 1945, when I was 23, I anticipated these questions, even if in a deceptively positive way:

> At times one wrestles with the question whether to interpret the events of the breakthrough as insanity, steps toward integration, or true mystic revelation. For me they were all three. When a person with as much basic energy as I have nevertheless has a small and unintegrated self that blocks the free flow of that energy, tensions are built up that might produce insanity. However, the release of those tensions is also a necessary prelude to the integration of the self and the spontaneous activity that should follow that integration. Finally the integration is not an end in itself, but a means whereby one goes inward to the realization of God-within and outward to meet the Eternal Thou in others and in the world.

Reflecting on these experiences many years later, I wrote in *Touchstones of Reality* that I carried with me back into the world a deep confusion, as one of my "touchstones of reality" broke up or gave way to another until finally they all ceased to be lifeways for me.

> I was left with unanswerable questions as to what in all that I had experienced was real and what was self-deception, or even delusion, in which intensity and the release of repressed forces masqueraded as personal wholeness, and irresistible compulsion masqueraded as the "will of God." Intensity, I soon recognized, often seems to be wholeness because it helps us look away from those anxieties in ourselves that we are afraid to face.[2]

I have often delighted in George Santayana's definition of a fanatic as a person who redoubles his efforts as he loses sight of his goal!

I have been helped in these confusions as I have gradually reached a personal wholeness that, if never sure or complete, nonetheless can grow from one moment of meeting to the next so that we can live with what Buber in *The Way of Man* calls a "relaxed vigilance." I have been helped too by Buber's understanding of genuine decision, not as the clenched fist and the set jaw that imposes one part of the person on the other but as the "rapture" that gives all of our passions direction in response to situation and event.

Leslie H. Farber, the distinguished psychoanalyst, has elaborated this distinction in his writings in the form of a contrast between *will* and *willfulness*. True *will* he defines as an appropriate alternation between the unconscious will of the first realm, the will of the whole being, and the conscious will of the second realm, the will of deliberate decision. *Willfulness*, in contrast, is the attempt of the will of the second realm to do the work of the first — to ape spontaneity, wholeness, strength.[3] Seen from both Buber's and Farber's points of view, there need be no conflict between spontaneity and genuine decision because genuine decision means decision of the whole being and as such includes our spontaneity. When will and spontaneity are in conflict, it is always really willfulness that is in question, the willfulness that wants to handle both sides of the dialogue. The will that helps us grow, religiously and otherwise, is that of the person whose trust is grounded in the partnership of existence. But the will that sees everything as depending on it alone, easily falls into despair when it cannot "master" the situation.

The same is true of our awareness of ourselves. True self-awareness does not turn us into objects through reflection and analysis. Rather, it is an intuitive awareness of ourselves that grows in listening and responding if we use ourselves as a radar screen: hearing not just how the other responds but also how we ourselves respond to the other. "Our wholeness is most there when we have forgotten ourselves in responding fully to what is not ourselves," I wrote in *Touchstones of Reality*:

> It is not just *ekstasis*, mystic ecstasy, that occasionally lifts us out of the burden of self-consciousness. Any genuine

wholehearted response — "When the music is heard so deeply that you are the music while the music lasts" — can bring us to this immediacy. Our self-consciousness returns when we go back, as we must, from immediacy to mediacy. Yet even it need not get in the way as much as we usually suppose. The fact that we are reflective can be handled lightly instead of heavily, especially if we do not make the mistake of identifying our "I" with that reflective consciousness and regarding the rest as just the objects that the "I" looks at.... One of the forms of lack of personal wholeness, correspondingly, is that endless self-preoccupation which splits us into two parts, one of which is the observer and the other the actor who is being observed. This bifurcation of consciousness prevents us from having any sort of spontaneous response, from ever really going outside of ourselves.[4]

If there is a danger of mistaking intensity for personal wholeness, there is also a danger of mistaking personal wholeness, at those rare moments when we attain it, for the "will of God." This danger is intensified if we begin with a philosophy of religion that makes us seek totally to lose or annihilate the self and to become either one with God or an instrument of his will. A striking modern example of this is Eliot's *Murder in the Cathedral*. In this work, as we have seen, Eliot imposes on his audience an objective, universal, and sacred design that it must accept, and he makes of his central figure the main spokesman for that design. In his long speeches toward the end, Thomas claims that he now has no will of his own, that he has become entirely an instrument of God to carry out God's objective design. Identifying himself with objective reality, he thinks he is acting in complete humility precisely at the point where he has projected his own point of view onto the universe at large. To do this is to deny the self-evident ground on which one stands — the inescapable reality of one's own particular existence and one's own point of view.

This pseudo-objectivity stands in marked contrast to the great religious figures of the world's history — Job contending with God, St. Francis receiving the stigmata in passionate love for Christ, the Buddha stubbornly persevering until he attains his own enlightenment in his own way, and Jesus in the Garden of Gethsemane praying, "Father if it be Thy will, may this cup be taken from me. Nevertheless, not my will but Thine be done." There is no question in each of these cases that there is a real self, a genuine existential subject over against the divine.[5]

Another equally striking example is found in the writings of the twentieth-century mystic, saint, and gnostic, Simone Weil, who in her teaching of *Waiting for God* insists on a total suspension of our own thoughts so that we might be "ready to receive in its named truth the object that is to penetrate it." Warmth of heart, impulsiveness, pity will not make up for a lack of this kind of *attention*. Though it alone can we receive into ourselves the being that we are looking at, "just as he is, in all his truth." Weil goes so far as to demand that it "be publicly and officially recognized that religion is nothing else but a looking" — a curiously strident insistence for one who holds religion to be waiting, openness, and receptivity! There is, indeed, something paradoxical in the humility that leads Weil to a complete denial of self in favor of objectivity and at the same time makes possible the most dogmatic and intolerant pronouncements on every subject. Weil wished to destroy her *I* and attain the plane of pure truth and pure objectivity. But there is another *I* that she identified with this plane and, so far from destroying it, she set it no practical limits. She found her *I* by denying it, found it, in fact, in a much more absolute way than would be possible for a person who admitted that her own subjectivity entered into her relation to the truth that she possessed.[6]

Our concern with wholeness and decision and with finding in every situation the right interrelation between structure and spontaneity issues, in the end, into a philosophy of action. One's reason, one's motivation, one's relation to an action determine its very nature, quality, and effectiveness. Karma yoga — the yoga of action — is action without attachment to the fruits of action. You live in the world and act, but you are not acting for the sake of the result. If you want to help others, you can only do so out of your spiritual state of being. And yet you cannot cultivate that state of being in order to help others. If you do so, you will be thinking of the fruit of the action, and therefore your state of being will not be that out of which effective help can proceed. This is a paradox. But this is the only true, the only effective action, according to the Gita. Søren Kierkegaard, in his beautiful book *Purity of Heart is to Will One Thing*, says that one should be like a man taking aim and that one should concentrate upon the aim and not the goal. In Eugen Herrigel's *Zen and the Art of Archery*, we find the identical point of view as the real secret of the Zen approach to archery: one does not try to attain something by looking at the target, the goal. One concentrates on "the means whereby" — to use the phrase of F. M. Alexander — and the means is no mere technique, but includes the very spirit of the doing.

In our philosophy of action Lao-tzu needs the counterbalancing of Confucius with his emphasis upon structure and conscious intention and the recognition that, because people do not reveal their feelings, the only safe guide is not to do to others what you would not want done to yourself. In some moments of life it is structure that counts and at others flowing. "The way of life" is a swinging interaction of the love in which structure is both created and informed by flowing, flowing both preserved and facilitated by structure. Lao-tze, nonetheless, has the deeper insight into the willing of the whole being that, in its openness and response, means spontaneity as opposed to the willfulness that tries to impose itself upon others.

12

World View and Existential Trust

Every lock has its key which is fitted to it and opens it. But there are strong thieves who know how to open without keys. They break the lock. So every mystery in the world can be unriddled by the particular kind of meditation fitted to it. But God loves the thief who breaks the lock open: I mean the man who breaks his heart for God.

I do not beg you to reveal to me the secret of your ways — I could not bear it! But show me one thing; show it to me more clearly and more deeply: show me what this, which is happening at this very moment, means to me, what it demands of me, what you, Lord of the world, are telling me by way of it. Ah, it is not why I suffer, that I wish to know, but only whether I suffer for your sake.

> The surest test if a man be sane
> Is if he accepts life whole, as it is,
> Without needing by measure or touch to understand
> The measureless untouchable source
> Of its images,
> The measureless untouchable source
> Of its substances,
> The source which, while it appears dark emptiness,
> Brims with a quick force
> Farthest away
> And yet nearest at hand
> From oldest time unto this day,

Charging its images with origin:
What more need I know of the origin
than this?[1]

They build their ark and name it *Weltanschauung* and seal up
with pitch not only its cracks but also its windows in order to shut
out the waters of the living world.

— Martin Buber, *Daniel*

THE ALTERNATION between immediacy and mediacy, between
dialogue and objectification makes up our existence and our
religious way. Ultimately, however, we must choose —
whether to enregister everything in some comprehensive *gnosis*
or to take our stand on an existential trust that cannot pretend
to get its arms around the creation on which it stands.

From the standpoint of existential trust, the oneness of God is
not a superabstraction but the renewed meeting with the ever
unique and the ever particular. "God-talk" is objective,
"experience-talk" is subjective. Touchstones of reality point
beyond both to the knowing of dialogue, of mutual contact.
Touchstones have less to do with what we *think* about walking
our daily lives than with the walking itself.

There is a tendency to confuse two different kinds of meaning
— a comprehensive world view, or *Weltanschauung*, which
gives us a sense of intellectual security, and the meaning that
arises moment by moment through our meeting with a reality
that we cannot embrace. Many people when they have a
religious or mystical experience move quickly to a metaphysics
and identify their experience with one particular philosophy of
religion or of mysticism. Not content with having found
meaning in immediacy, they want to wrap up reality in some
conceptual totality. Perhaps one of the most important witnesses
that can be made in our day is that it is not necessary to have a
Weltanschauung, a comprehensive world view, in order to be
able to live as a human being. This means, in terms of theology,
that our stance, our life-attitude, is more basic than the
affirmation or nonaffirmation of a Being or ground of being. No
intellectual construction, not even the philosophy of dialogue,
can ever include the real otherness of the other. In meeting the
other, I come up against something absurd in the root meaning

of the term — something irreducible that I cannot register in my categories. A God I could meet apart from my meeting with otherness might be a God-idea but not the true God.

A world view is like a geodesic dome. It creates a special atmosphere for you, keeps certain air currents up, and gives you a sense of spaciousness without giving you the real world where the winds blow freely and sometimes uncomfortably. A world view exists within your consciousness, even when you share it with any number of other persons. No matter how adequate the world view is, it leaves out otherness by definition. For that is the very nature of the other — that it cracks and destroys every *Weltanschauung*, that it does not fit into any ensemble of coherences, that it is absurd. There is something about the whole enterprise of theology, metaphysics, and often of philosophy of religion that tempts the thinker to see God, humanity, and the world as if from above and to leave herself or himself out of it, making us wonder where the thinker got the vantage point through which she or he could transcend the dialectic between God and the world and see it as a whole! We meet the eternal Thou only in our existence as persons, only in our meeting with the other. We cannot know it from outside existence. This means renouncing the attempt to include God in any conceptual system, including the process philosophies of Whitehead, Hartshorne, and Teilhard de Chardin. It is not insight into process but trust in existence that ultimately enables us to enter into genuine meeting with the unique reality that accosts us in each new moment.

There is, to be sure, a relation between our truths — our touchstones of reality — both those we experience in our own lives and those we encounter in the lives of others. But this is not a relation of abstract and timeless consistency. Rather our old touchstones can be reaffirmed in each new situation — not as the same but as illuminated and transformed by the new. We do not *have* truth. We have, moment by moment, a relationship to truth. In each new discovery or rediscovery our earlier touchstones are brought into the fullness of the present. This we can affirm, but we must avoid the illusion that in our concrete existence we can rise to a reference point above the dimension of time — an abstract spatiality divorced from events. Hence the *re-cognition of God* and the *re-affirmation of truth* are ultimately the same: both are known again in concrete uniqueness, not in abstract sameness. This leads us to a *hierarchy of criteria of truth*. Objectivizing, structuring, formulating are essential in carrying forward our truths, but if we content ourselves with them alone, we lose our touchstones. We must take the further step of bringing the old touchstones into the new. Therefore, our *ultimate criterion of meaning and truth is not the objectification of a structure but the lived new meeting with reality*.

It may help us to distinguish between two different meanings of the phrase *ground of being*. One of these is found in conceptual, or ontological, formulations. The other is a ground only in the sense of what we can touch on in our situation, in our experience, in our existence — what gives us the courage to take a step forward and then perhaps another step forward and still another. With the former meaning of ground, I can have nothing to do because it presupposes getting behind or above creation, going beyond the given of our existence, of our finite freedom and our both finite and infinite knowing. The other meaning of ground of being I can and do affirm, for this is precisely what I mean by touchstones of reality. Existential trust has to do with this second meaning, but not necessarily and often not at all with the first. Existential trust does not depend upon the conscious affirmation of belief in the existence of God, for what a person believes, in the conscious, rational sense of that term, often has little or even a negative connection with his or her basic life-attitude.

The great Protestant theologian Paul Tillich offers an excellent example of *both* uses of ground of being. Sometimes he seems to want to impose acceptance of the term through logic and other times he makes it a witness of faith and trust. Tillich wishes to go beyond the divine Thou that is encountered by Kierkegaard to the transpersonal "ground of being itself." "The theologians who speak so strongly and with such self-certainty about the divine-human encounter should be aware of a situation in which this encounter is prevented by radical doubt and nothing is left but absolute faith." The courage to be takes radical doubt, the doubt about God, into itself, and makes God into a living God — the self-affirmation of Being itself which prevails against non-being. Tillich sees the "personal" God of theological theism as "a being beside others and as such a part of the whole of reality." At the same time, this limited God is the subject that makes us into objects and deprives us of our freedom as persons by his omnipotence and omniscience.

The only alternative that Tillich sees to the despair of atheistic existentialism that God's all-powerfulness produces is transcending theism in "absolute faith." Kierkegaard's I-Thou relation to the God of theism cannot enable one to take the anxiety of doubt and meaninglessness into the courage to be. But mysticism, too, must be transcended; for "mysticism does not take seriously the concrete and the doubt concerning the concrete" — the world of finite values and meanings. The divine-human encounter is paradoxical, however; for in it the God above the God of theism is present, although hidden. It is the Thou, but it is also nearer to the I than the I is to itself. Here, personalism and the transpersonal go hand in hand — so well indeed that one wonders why Tillich need posit the "God above God" as a separate logical or theological category. Knowing for Tillich is knowing in the relationship of faith, but at a still deeper level, it is the knowledge that gives the ground for that relationship. To this extent, Tillich shores up the existential encounter with God with the essentialist gnosis that takes refuge in comprehensive concepts.

The question that this faith in a comprehensive system of knowledge raises has never been posed more sharply than by Tillich's disciple and friend, David E. Roberts:

> I have always been mystified as to how he could be so flex-ible, concrete, vital, and "close to home" on the one hand, and so schematic, abstract, abstruse, and remote on the other.... The schematic aspect ... is an asset wherever it is used analytically and organizationally, that is, where it is used to clarify concepts and to show their interrelatedness. But it becomes a liability at the point where existential problems, after being highlighted, are swallowed into an abyss. Somehow Tillich, like God, manages to engulf dis-tinctions without blurring them. He fully realizes (again, no doubt, like God) that such problems are met, insofar as

they ever are, by living rather than by constructing systems. But it is a weird experience, which I have undergone many times, to have problems answered with great sensitivity and patience, by being brought into connection with some relevant segment of the system, only to discover later that I do not happen to be the man who carries this system around in his head.[2]

Existentialism, which begins with a reaction against Hegel's universal system, is always in danger — either by way of philosophy or by way of theology — of ending by incorporating its insights into some new Hegelian dialectic. The reaction against system ends in system. The reaction against *Weltanschauung* ends in *Weltanschauung!*

Yet the ground of being for Tillich is not merely a logical, theological, or metaphysical concept. It is also a living presence that undergirds the relation between the I and the Thou, whether the latter be divine or human. In that sense it is identical with touchstones of reality and with existential trust. Thus at the end of *The Courage to Be*, the very book in which he writes about the necessity of going beyond the I-Thou relationship to the God above God, Tillich movingly witnesses:

> Absolute faith, or the state of being grasped by the God beyond God, is not a state which appears beside other states of the mind. It never is something separated and definite, an event which could be isolated and described. It is always a movement in, with, and under other states of the mind. It is the situation on the boundary of man's possibilities. It *is* this boundary. Therefore it is both the courage of despair and the courage in and above every courage. It is not a place where one can live, it is without the safety of words and concepts, it is without a name, a church, a cult, a theology. But it is moving in the depth of all of them. It is the power of being, in which they participate and of which they are fragmentary expressions.[3]

Although in his book *Biblical Religion and the Search for Ultimate Reality* Tillich says against Pascal (and therefore by implication against Buber) that the God of the Philosophers and the

God of Abraham, Isaac, and Jacob are the same God, much that Tillich says in that book is very close to Buber's own understanding of God as the "absolute Person who *is* not a person but becomes one, so to speak, in order to know and be known, to love and be loved by man." "Man can experience the holy in and through everything," writes Tillich, "but as the holy, it cannot be less than he is; it cannot be a-personal."

> It is the unconditional character of the biblical God that makes the relation to him radically personal. For only that which concerns us in the center of our personal existence concerns us unconditionally. The God who is unconditional in power, demand, and promise is the God who makes us completely person and who, consequently, is completely personal in our encounter with him.[4]

At the same time, Tillich reaffirms that the God who is a being is transcended by the God who is Being itself, the ground and abyss of every being. But he also asserts, in language very like that of Buber's "absolute Person," that "the God who is *a* person is transcended by the God who is the Personal-itself, the ground and abyss of every person." His conclusion is that the ground of being is the ground of personal being, not its negation.

> Religiously speaking, this means that our encounter with the God who is a person includes the encounter with the God who is the ground of everything personal and as such not *a* person. . . . The I-thou character of the relation never darkens the transpersonal power and mystery of the divine.[5]

Tillich, nonetheless, does not see the necessity of an ultimate choice between existential trust and gnosis, as Buber does in his contrast between gnosis and *devotio*. This contrast between Tillich and Buber is not unlike Buber's contrast between Hasidism and the Kabbalah. The Kabbalah schematizes the mystery, Buber said, whereas Hasidism stops short, cowers in terror, and lets itself be disconcerted. I can think of no better illustration of this than Rabbi Zusya in a story entitled "The Fear of God":

> Once Zusya prayed to God: "Lord, I love you so much, but I do not fear you enough! Lord, I love you so much, but I

do not fear you enough! Let me stand in awe of you like your angels, who are penetrated by your awe-inspiring name." And God heard his prayer, and his name penetrated the hidden heart of Zusya as it does those of the angels. But Zusya crawled under the bed like a little dog, and animal fear shook him until he howled: "Lord, let me love you like Zusya again!" And God heard him this time also.[6]

Once, without being aware of it, I strove to push Buber into the affirmation of a metaphysical doctrine to underline his trust in redemption. In the Martin Buber section of *Philosophical Interrogations*, I asked him whether the relation to the eternal Thou includes not only the temporal I-Thou relation but the I-It relation, too? What is more, I supported this question with impressive testimony from Buber's own writing in *I and Thou* where he speaks of the primal twofold movement of "estrangement from" and "turning toward" the primal Source:

> Every real relation in the world is consummated in the interchange of actual and potential being, but in pure relation — in the relation of man to God — potential is still actual being. . . . By virtue of this great privilege of pure relation there exists the unbroken world of Thou which binds up the isolated moments of relation in a life of world solidarity.[7]

Does this not mean, I asked Buber, that we relate to the actual and present eternal Thou even when the temporal Thou has again become only past and potential, that is, when it has again become It?. Is it not through a *continuing* relation with the eternal Thou that we are able ever again to find the Thou, either with the person who was Thou for us but is now It, or with some other whom we have never before met as Thou? If we know the unique value of another only in the I-Thou relationship, is it not the potentiality of his being, or again being a Thou for us, that ultimately prevents our treating the person whom we do not know as Thou purely as a dispensable It? And does not that person's "potential Thou" rest not only on the "actual Thou" of remembered I-Thou relationhips, but on the actual Thou of Present Reality — the relation to the eternal Thou "in which potential is still actual being"? Is it not our trust in the eternal Thou that gives actuality and continuity to our discontinuous and often merely potential relations to the human Thou?

Buber's response, like that of Zusya, was a drawing back, a stopping short, an allowing himself to be disconcerted. He declined to back up his earlier words in such a way as to allow me to discern a gnosis underlying his existential trust:

> I perceive in this question, from words of mine which have been quoted here, that I have already come close to the limit of what is accessible to our experience. I hesitate to go a step further with words the full responsibility for which I cannot bear. *In our experience* our relation to God does *not* include our I-It relations. What is the case beyond our experience, thus so to speak, from the side of God, no longer belongs to what can be discussed. Perhaps I have here and there, swayed by the duty of the heart that bids me point out what I have to point out, already said too much.[8]

Almost 15 years later, when I wrote *Touchstones of Reality*, I no longer sought to espy in the eternal Thou some ground of being that would give continuity and security to our discontinuous and insecure meetings with the Thou and our equally discontinuous and unsafeguarded touchstones of reality. Instead I pointed out that, in order to make existential trust real in our lives, we need the courage to address and the courage to respond. I find these terms more concrete and helpful than Paul Tillich's "courage to be." The courage to address and respond means the courage to go out to meet the reality given in this moment, whatever its form, because here only is meaning accessible to us. We are not placed first of all before Camus' question, "Shall I commit suicide in the face of the absurd?" or before Tillich's question, "Can I affirm non-being in order to be able to participate in being?" but before the question, "Do I have the courage to go out to meet and respond to what comes to meet me?" This includes the courage *not* to speak and *not* to respond when we are "triggered off" rather than really addressed in our whole beings.

This courage is identical with existential trust. It cannot be attained by "positive thinking" nor does it lead to "peace of mind" or "peace of soul." It is not disconsonant with pain, grief, anxiety, vulnerability, and the Dialogue with the Absurd. Where it has been sapped by existential mistrust, one no longer goes forth to meet others. "The broken heart it kens nae second spring again thae the waeful nae cease frae their greeting," goes "Loch Lomond." Or as the poet Conrad Aiken puts it, "Is there no one to cry 'forsaken!' for those who creep through life guarding the heart from blows to die obscurely?' Often our past experiences of being unconfirmed or given the cold shoulder make us give way before the meeting with the present. Yet more than we can conceive, we are sustained from within ourselves, from what comes to meet us, and from the meeting itself. The smog of existential mistrust need not prevent ever-new contact with reality. If we dare to trust, we may grow in the courage to address and the courage to respond. More than this is not asked of us.

The reality of creation is the reality of the otherness that we cannot remove into our rational comprehension of the world. We seek to anthropomorphize creation — to rationalize reality to fit our moral conceptions. Despite our power to comprehend the world, it has a reality independent of us. The real God is not the God whom man removes into the sphere of his own spirit and thought, but the creator who speaks to man through creatures that exist for their own sake and not just for human purposes. The meaning of the life of dialogue, similarly, is not what we get from God — whether it be "peace of mind," "peace of soul," "successful living," or "positive thinking" — but our walking with God on this earth. The trust at the heart of this walking with God is tried and we are exiled by the passage of time, by sickness and death, and by the very social order that we build. There is the possibility of renewing this trust, but only if we can bring the exile into the dialogue with God, not if we turn away from the exile or overlook it. What happened to Job can and does happen, in more or less concentrated form, to any human being. Instead of turning Job's situation into the abstract metaphysical problem of evil, we should encounter it as a touchstone of reality. For the real question — the question that lies at the inmost core of our very existence — is not *Why?* but *How?* How can we live in a world in which Auschwitz and Hiroshima happen? How can we find the resources once more to go out to a meeting with the new moment?

13

Is Religion the Enemy of Mankind?

A certain man was believed to have died, and was being prepared for burial, when he revived.

He sat up, but he was so shocked at the scene surrounding him that he fainted.

He was put in a coffin, and the funeral party set off for the cemetery.

Just as they arrived at the grave, he regained consciousness, lifted the coffin lid, and cried out for help.

"It is not possible that he has revived," said the mourners, "because he has been certified dead by competent experts."

"But I am alive!" shouted the man.

He appealed to a well-known and impartial scientist and jurisprudent who was present.

"Just a moment," said the expert.

He then turned to the mourners, counting them. "Now, we have heard what the alleged deceased has had to say. You fifty witnesses tell me what you regard as the truth."

"He is dead," said the witnesses.

"Bury him!" said the expert.

And so he was buried.

If someone comes to you and asks your help, you shall not turn him off with pious words, saying: "Have faith and take your troubles to God!" You shall act as if there were no God, as if there were only one person in all the world who could help this man — only yourself.

Whoever says that the words of the Torah are one thing and the words of the world another, must be regarded as a man who denies God.[1]

"R ELIGION," MARTIN BUBER once wrote, "is the great enemy of mankind." He was speaking, of course, of religion when it is used to perpetuate the dualism between the spirit and the everyday and as such becomes a threat to human wholeness. Human wholeness, from the perspective of touchstones of reality, is not simply inner individuation or integration but the wholeness of persons within the partnership of existence, and *that* finds its most meaningful form in the "community of otherness." If we look at our question from this standpoint, we must confess that just as the structures of society more often block the way to genuine community than promote it, so also the structures of religion — creed, cult, and church — more often further a community of affinity, or likemindedness, than they do a community of otherness. What is more, by its very claim to have a corner on the spirit and by the tendency to regard religion as the refuge from the mundane world, religious institutions and groups more often intensify the dualism between spirit and world than overcome it.

The other side of this paradox is that in a secular society, which in its ever greater complexity is of necessity more and more compartmentalized, religion is perhaps the one human activity and concern that might bring the disparate spheres into healing contact with one another and guard thereby the wholeness of the human. A humanist might protest that this could also be done without religion, and I would not deny it. Yet by and large it is not done. What is more, by and large the problem is not even seen as a problem because people seem quite content to divide their lives into compartments that have little to do with one another.

Many years ago I went to a party at the Greenwich Village apartment of a Harvard classmate and friend. It was not too large an apartment or too large a party, yet it broke up "naturally" into clusters — one of his Harvard friends, one of his high school friends, one of those he knew at summer camp, one of his

Is Religion the Enemy of Mankind? • 183

fellow workers at *Time, Life,* and *Sports Illustrated,* one of
Greenwich Village's musicians and composers. My friend moved
from group to group talking briefly with each. It struck me at the
time that this was an exact microcosm of New York City itself
with its many cultures that pass by one another without meeting. In a considerably smaller city, such as San Diego, one might
imagine there would be only one culture. Yet I was similarly
struck recently when I emerged from a breathtakingly beautiful
performance of the Bach B Minor Mass in the wonderful Immac-
ulata Cathedral of the University of San Diego and passed by the
San Diego Stadium where the Padres or the Chargers were enact-
ing a very different sort of rite! What, I wondered, could bring
these two cultures together?

If this is true among groups of people, it is also true within individuals themselves. Each of us has so many different associa-
tions in so many different contexts that without realizing it we
become accustomed to shifting gears with each one.
Occasionally I have difficulty recognizing not only voices over
the telephone but also names unless I can place first the context
of the person who is speaking. Not so long ago I wrote a doctor-
al student at the University of Utah, whom I had met only once,
asking her if she could send me a picture of herself with her next
chapter. An image of another woman had intervened, and I
could neither locate the image nor get it out of my mind. In en-
deavoring to place it, I methodically went over what turned out
to be an incredible number of different places and contexts with
which I had been associated in the last 20 years only to realize
finally that the image was of someone I know here and now!

Neither human existence nor religion can exist in pure immediacy. The history of religion is far more a history of objective
structures of creed, cult, and grouping than of direct revelations,
theophanies, ecstasies, or dialogues between man and the divine.
To acknowledge this dialectic still leaves unanswered the question of which is the master and which is the servant, which the
end and which the means. Insofar as religions become bastions
to protect the spirit against defilement by the world or to protect
the community of believers from contact with those who do not
believe in the same way, then we must say that structure and

objectification are the master and that religion is, indeed, the enemy of mankind. This is not just a question of how we define religion but of what is the prevailing tendency or direction within any given religious life, religious group, religious institution, or religious tradition.

In response to the question whether one should pay taxes to the Roman government, Jesus asked whose picture was on the coin and then answered, "Render unto Caesar the things that are Caesar's and unto God the things that are God's." Assuming this to be an authentic saying growing out of a specific historical, political, and economic context, we cannot fail to note how often the same question has been asked in effect in the ages since. Not long after the death of Jesus, Rabbi Akiba was burned at the stake by the Romans for his persistence in practising and teaching Judaism, which the Romans had outlawed in Palestine. When his disciples exclaimed at the look of joy on his face, he said, "All my life I have wanted to recite the *Sh'ma* [Hear O Israel, the Lord Our God, the Lord is One.] in the right way, and now I can do so!" This became the origin of the designation of martyrdom within Judaism as the *Kiddush Ha-Shem*, the sanctification of the name of God, a sanctification that not only means declaring God's oneness but also *yihud*, the practical task of unification in the face of the monstrous contradictions of life.

Not long after the martyrdom of Akiba and other Jewish rabbis, countless Christians were martyred in Rome for their insistence on continuing their Christianity and for their refusal to take part in the army or own slaves or otherwise serve the Roman Empire, which they identified with the Great Beast of the Apocalypse. Yet from the time of Constantine on, the Church and the State became identified and Jesus' saying about the tribute money was increasingly used as a justification for that very dualism between spirit and life that made Buber speak of religion as the great enemy of mankind.

What seems the self-evident meaning of the saying is not necessarily the real one, however, as Buber himself has pointed out in "The Validity and Limitation of the Political Principle," a speech that he gave at the German universities at the time when he first consented to appear publicly in the post-war Germany, which until then had appeared to him "faceless" because of the 12 years of Nazi totalitarianism. In the two millenia since Jesus answered this question, the particular situations out of which it arises have become ever more difficult and contradictory, even though it is often not one of foreign rule but one's own and not of a government sustained by force but one willingly submitted to. In an age where everything else is made relative, the political principle and with it the sovereignty of each separate nation has been made absolute. In the political state, and especially in its highest fulfillment, the totalitarian state, what man owes to Caesar is simply himself and what is left over for God is virtually nothing. Hegel, Marx, and Heidegger each in his own way have absolutized history and the historical state and have attributed to the state the legitimately unconditional determining force. As a result, the state comes to occupy the divine seat of authority — until, as inevitably happens, the plurality of states and the uneasy balance of power set a limit from without to the absolutism within.

The choice is not between being a "Single One" in the style of Kierkegaard or submerging oneself in a party or a state, but rather between serving a Mammon that swallows up the soul and leaves nothing of it free and serving the group *quantum satis* — as much as is possible and desirable at any one time and in any given conflict without surrendering to it once and for all. "In each situation that demands decision the demarcation line between service and service must be drawn anew — not necessarily with fear, but necessarily with that trembling of the soul that precedes every genuine decision." One can serve God within the party and the state, but only by drawing the demarcation line ever anew and that means above all by not giving over the integrity of oneself and one's cause in the name of the end justifying the means:

> What is at stake here is shown most clearly when means are proposed whose nature contradicts the nature of the goal. Here, too, one is obliged not to proceed on principle, but only to advance ever again in the responsibility of the line of demarcation and to answer for it; not in order to keep one's soul clean of blood — that would be a vain and

wretched enterprise — but in order to guard against means
being chosen that will lead away from the cherished goal to
another goal essentially similar to those means; for the end
never sanctifies the means, but the means can certainly
thwart the end.[2]

What Buber concludes from this is that those who, however various their goals, are united in their fidelity to the truth of God,
must unite to give to God what is God's, or what, in our day,
may come to the same thing — to give to man what is man's in
order to save him from being devoured by the political principle.

If we look closely at what Buber has said, we shall see that he
has proceeded by a different logic than those who take it for
granted that Jesus meant that one should give one part of human
existence, the material, to Caesar, and another part, the spiritual, to God. The real contrast here is between the part and the
whole; for the structures of economics and the state are always
structures of the part, structures of indirectness and mediacy,
whereas the realm and claim of God is always the whole that, if
anything can, legitimizes those partial structures and imparts
meaning to them.

Looked at in this way, the question of whether religion is an
enemy to mankind is not a question that can be answered in
general, academically, or once for all, say, from the outside by
its opponents or from within by its proponents. It can only be
answered again and again, in each situation of trust and contending anew, by those of us who fight on whatever front, within whatever group, or even — like Luther, Socrates, and Amos
— alone! It is we who decide in each new battlefield whether the
prevailing direction of religion is toward a dualism in which the
spirit has no binding claim upon life and life falls apart into un-
hallowed segments or toward the continual overcoming of that
dualism by taking up again and again the task of hallowing the
creation that has been given to us. Every rung of human existence can be a ground of hallowing if we put off the habitual. The
religious person meets God, not in the aseity of the philosophers,
but in the events and meetings of concrete life, in the Dialogue
with the Absurd.

Each religious person has his or her own touchstones and the emphases that his or her tradition and situation make necessary. No philosopher of religion has the right to prescribe ideal requisites for the coming of the kingdom. There is, nonetheless, a direction of movement within each tradition and between and among traditions, groups, and individual persons that might enhance the partnership of existence and the mutually confirming dialogue of touchstones of reality.

The first element of that direction is fervor. We do not need a "religious revival" nor certainly any turning away from study or from the full and, where possible, improved, use of our powers of reason. But we do need genuine fervor if religion is to call to the wholeness of the person and the community and help them to find the ever-renewed direction toward God amid the complexities and contradictions of the present.

A second element is genuine community, the movement toward a community of otherness, first within the religious group itself, and then between group and group, culture and culture, nation and nation, people and people — openhearted dialogue that confirms the other in his or her otherness and does not demand that the word or way of the other conform to one's own.

A third element is the overcoming of dualism by the insistence, in each human and social sphere anew, that the spirit be relevant to life and that life be open to the demand of the spirit. Only thus can the mediate and indirect structures of our existence be brought into the immediate and be given meaning by the whole.

Lastly, and perhaps in this hour most important, is the recovery of existential trust through the courage to address and the courage to respond. This is the *Via Humana*, the Human Way, the "life of dialogue" in which our dialogue with one another and our dialogue with the absurd issue ever anew into our meeting with the eternal Thou. The awareness of the ineffable is included within this dialogue: for it means nothing other than true openness to the wonder met in every moment. The dialogue of touchstones opens to us a different way of living, a greater wholeness, than the compartmentalization of our lives into inner and outer, feeling and thought, subjective and objective, individual and society, can ever do.

The only perennial philosophy that I can and do espouse is that of openness — the witness to the ever-growing dialogue with committed persons of every religion and none. Each of the religions and each of the touchstones that I have entered into dialogue with have pointed me toward greater openness, and each has opened for comrades on the way the possibility of a fuller and freer fellowship — a mutually confirming dialogue of touchstones.

Only we can remove from our eyes that one small hand that shuts off from us the enormous lights and mysteries which fill the world. Only we can bring to light the hidden human image — the image of the imageless God.

Whoever says that the words of the Torah are one thing and the words of the world another must be regarded as a person who denies God.

Notes

Chapter 2 — The Insight of the Religions into the Problem of Human Existence

1. This chapter is based upon Chapters 6-9 of Maurice Friedman, *Touchstones of Reality: Existential Trust and the Community of Peace* (New York: E. P. Dutton, 1972, Dutton Books [paperback], 1974), pp. 85-204.

Chapter 4 — The *Via Humana*

1. Martin Buber, *Tales of the Hasidim: The Early Masters*, trans. by Olga Marx (New York: Schocken Books, 1961), "To Say Torah and to be Torah," p. 107; Martin Buber, *Tales of the Hasidim: The Later Masters*, trans. by Olga Marx (New York: Schocken Books, 1961), "Holiness," p. 281.

2. Buber, *Tales of the Hasidim: The Later Masters*, "It Is I," p. 261.

3. Martin Buber, *The Prophetic Faith*, trans. from the Hebrew by Carlyle Witton-Davies (New York: Harper Torchbooks, 1960), p. 111.

Chapter 5 — Legend, Myth, and Tale; Religion and Literature

1. Buber, *Tales of the Hasidim: The Early Masters*, Preface, p. v f.

2. Ernst Cassirer, *Language and Myth*, trans. by Suzanne Langer (New York: Harper and Brothers, 1946), pp. 11, 18, 27.

3. H. and H. A. Frankfort, *et al.*, *The Intellectual Adventure of Ancient Man: An Essay on Speculative Thought in the Ancient Near East* (Chicago: University of Chicago Press, 1946), p. 4 ff. and concluding chapter, "The Emancipation of Thought from Myth," which is also found in H. and H. A. Frankfort, *et al.*, *Before Philosophy*, Chapter 8 (New York: Penguin Books), pp. 241-48.

4. Martin Buber, *The Prophetic Faith*, p. 46.

5. Martin Buber, *Hasidism and Modern Man*, ed. and trans. with an Introduction by Maurice Friedman (New York: Harper Torchbooks, 1966), p. 26.

6. Harry M. Buck, Jr., "From History to Myth: A Comparative Study," *The Journal of Bible and Religion*, Vol. XXIX, July 1961, p. 219 f.

7. Mircea Eliade, *Cosmos and History: The Myth of the Eternal Return*, trans. by Willard Trask (New York: Harper Torchbooks, 1959), p. 85.

8. *Ibid.*, p. 106 f.

9. *Ibid.*, p. 156.

10. *Ibid.*, p. 162.

11. *Ibid.*, p. 154 f.

12. *Ibid.*, p. 132.

13. Martin Buber, *Pointing the Way*, trans. and ed. by Maurice Friedman (New York: Schocken Books, 1974), "Prophecy, Apocalyptic, and the Historical Hour," p. 200. See pp. 192-207.

14. Martin Buber, *Israel and the World: Essays in A Time of Crisis* (New York: Schocken Books, 1963), "The Two Foci of the Jewish Soul," p. 36.

15. Eliade, *Cosmos and History*, p. 158 f.

16. For a fuller exposition see Maurice Friedman, *The Hidden Human Image* (New York: Delacorte Press, Delta Books [paperback], 1974), Chapter 6 — "Religion and Literature: Meeting or Mismeeting," pp. 93-105.

17. *Tales of the Hasidim: The Early Masters*, "How to Say Torah," p. 107.

Chapter 6 — Inwardness and the Life of Dialogue

1. Raymond Bernard Blakney, *Meister Eckhart. A Modern Translation* (New York: Harper Torchbooks, 1957), p. 14; Paul Reps, *Zen Flesh, Zen Bones: A Collection of Zen and Pre-Zen Writings* (New York: Doubleday, Anchor Books, 1961), "True Friends," p. 70 f.; *Tales of the Hasidim: The Early Masters*, "When Two Sing," p. 26.

2. Kenneth Boulding, *The Naylor Sonnets* (Nyack, New York: Fellowship Publications).

3. *Tales of the Hasidim: The Early Masters*, "Get Thee out of Thy Country," p. 244.

4. The preceding passages from Lao-tzu's teachings are quoted from *The Way of Life According to Lao-tzu*, trans. with an Introduction by Witter Bynner (New York: Capricorn Books, 1962), Passage Nos. 1, 7, 14, 47, 49.

Chapter 7 — The Partnership of Existence and the Dialogue of Touchstones

1. *Tales of the Hasidim: The Later Masters*, "Give and Take," p. 220; "How the Rabbi of Sasov Learned How to Love," p. 86.

2. Martin Buber, *The Knowledge of Man: A Philosophy of the Interhuman*, ed. with an Introductory Essay (Chapter 1) by Maurice Friedman (New York: Harper Torchbooks, 1966), "What Is Common to All," trans. by Maurice Friedman, p. 95 f.

3. *The Teachings of the Compassionate Buddha*, ed. with Introduction and Notes by Edwin A. Burtt (New York: New American Library, Mentor Books, 1955), p. 136.

4. *Lao Tzu / Tao Teh Ching*, trans. by John C. H. Wu, ed. by Paul K. T. Sih, Asian Institute Translations, No. 1 (New York: St. John's University Press,

1961), p. 17; *Chuang Tzu: Basic Writings*, trans. by Burton Watson (New York: Columbia University Press, 1964), p. 56 f.

5. *The Analects of Confucius*, trans. and annotated by Arthur Waley (New York: Vintage Books), pp. 162, 181, 189.

6. Martin Buber, *Between Man and Man*, trans. by Ronald Gregor Smith with an Introduction by Maurice Friedman (New York: Macmillan Books, 1965), "Dialogue," p. 7 f., italics added.

Chapter 8 — Peter Pan's Shadow: Tradition and Modernity

1. Mordecai Kaplan, *The Future of the American Jew* (New York: Macmillan, 1948), p. 35 f.

2. C. G. Jung, *Psychology and Alchemy, Collected Works*, Vol. XII (New York: Pantheon Books, 1953), p. 36.

3. C. G. Jung, *Aion: Researches into the Phenomenology of the Self, Collected Works*, Vol. IX (2) (New York: Pantheon Books, 1959), p. 70.

4. C. G. Jung, *Psychology and Religion: West and East, Collected Works*, Vol. XI, trans. by R. F. C. Hull (New York: Pantheon Books, 1958), pp. 82, 96, 157, italics added.

5. C. G. Jung, *Two Essays on Analytical Psychology, Collected Works*, Vol. VII (New York: Pantheon Books, 1953), p. 237.

6. C. G. Jung, *Answer to Job*, trans. by R. F. C. Hull (Cleveland and New York: World Publishing Co., 1960), pp. 179, 186.

7. For a full-scale treatment of Jung, see Maurice Friedman, *To Deny Our Nothingness: Contemporary Images of Man* (Chicago: University of Chicago Press, Phoenix Books, 1978), Chapter 9, pp. 146-167.

8. Maurice Friedman, *Touchstones of Reality*, Chapter 13, "Psychology and Religion: The Limits of the Psyche as A Touchstone of Reality," p. 250.

Chapter 9 — Dialectic of Spirit and Form

1. Thomas Merton, *The Way of Chuang Tzu* (New York: New Directions, 1965), "Three Friends," p. 54 f.

2. Paul Arthur Schilpp and Maurice Friedman, editors, *The Philosophy of Martin Buber* volume of *The Library of Living Philosophers* (LaSalle, Illinois: Open Court, 1967), Martin Buber, "Replies to My Critics," trans. by Maurice Friedman, p. 731.

3. Martin Buber, *Hasidism and Modern Man*, p. 25.

4. Israel J. Kazis, "Hasidism Re-examined," *The Reconstructionist*, Vol. XXIII, No. 8 (May 31, 1957), pp. 7-13.

Chapter 10 — The Paradox of Religious Leadership

1. Thomas Merton, *The Way of Chuang Tzu*, "The Sacrificial Swine," p. 108; Idries Shah, *The Way of the Sufi* (New York: E. P. Dutton [paperback], 1970), pp. 79 f., 149 f., 169; *Tales of the Hasidim: The Early Masters*, "Themselves," p. 48.

2. Based on Maurice Friedman, *To Deny Our Nothingness: Contemporary*

Images of Man, 3rd ed. with a new Preface and Appendix (Chicago: The University of Chicago Press, 1978), pp. 104-108.

3. Martin Buber, *Israel and the World*, "Biblical Leadership," p. 126.

4. *Ibid.*, p. 131.

5. *Ibid.*, p. 133.

6. Martin Buber, *Meetings*, ed. and trans. with an Introduction by Maurice Friedman (LaSalle, Illinois: Open Court Publishing Co., 1973), p. 37 f. Also found in Schilpp and Friedman, eds., *The Philosophy of Martin Buber*, p. 19.

7. Based on Maurice Friedman, *To Deny Our Nothingness*, p. 110.

8. *Ibid.*, p. 111 f.

9. Paul Reps, *Zen Flesh, Zen Bones*, "Right and Wrong," p. 41 f.

10. *Tales of the Hasidim: The Later Masters*, "Every Rabbi Is Good," p. 217.

11. Merton, *The Way of Chuang Tzu*, "Means and Ends," p. 154.

12. *Tales of the Hasidim: The Later Masters*, "Refusal," p. 126; *Zen Flesh, Zen Bones*, "What Are You Doing! What Are You Saying!" p. 59 f.

13. *Zen Flesh, Zen Bones*, "The Real Miracle," p. 68.

14. *Tales of the Hasidim: The Early Masters*, "The Strength of Community," p. 53 f.

Chapter 11 — Spontaneity, Decision, and Personal Wholeness

1. Merton, *The Way of Chuang Tzu*, "When Life Was Full there Was No History," p. 76; *Tales of the Hasidim: The Early Masters*, "The Hair Shirt," p. 153; *The Later Masters*, "The Enemy," p. 189; Martin Buber, *For the Sake of Heaven: A Chronicle*, trans. by Ludwig Lewisonn (New York: Atheneum, 1969), p. 6.

2. Maurice Friedman, *Touchstones of Reality*, pp. 67, 70.

3. Leslie H. Farber, *The Ways of the Will: Essays Toward A Psychology and Psychopathology of the Will* (New York: Basic Books, 1966); Leslie H. Farber, *lying, despair, jealousy, envy, sex, suicide, drugs, and the good life* (New York: Harper Colophon Books, 1978).

4. Maurice Friedman, *Touchstones of Reality*, p. 311 f.

5. Based on Maurice Friedman, *To Deny Our Nothingness*, p. 104 ff.

6. *Ibid.*, Chapter 8, pp. 135-45.

Chapter 12 — World View and Existential Trust

1. *Tales of the Hasidim: The Early Masters*, "The Strong Thief," p. 104; "Suffering and Prayer," p. 212 f.; Witter Bynner, *The Way of Life According to Lao Tzu*, No. 21, p. 37.

2. David E. Roberts, "Tillich's Doctrine of Man" in Charles W. Kegley and Robert W. Bretall, eds., *The Theology of Paul Tillich*, Vol. I of *The Library of Living Theologians* (New York: Macmillan, 1956), p. 130. Cf. Tillich's reply to Roberts on p. 329 f.

3. Paul Tillich, *The Courage to Be* (New York: Yale University Press, 1952; Yale Paperbounds, 1959), p. 188 f.

4. Paul Tillich, *Biblical Religion and the Search for Ultimate Reality* (Chicago: University of Chicago Press, 1955), p. 27.

5. *Ibid.*, pp. 81-85.

6. Martin Buber, *Tales of the Hasidim: The Early Masters*, p. 246.

7. Martin Buber, *I and Thou*, 2nd ed. with a Postscript by the author added, trans. by Ronald Gregor Smith (New York: Charles Scribner's Sons, 1958), p. 100.

8. Sydney and Beatrice Rome, editors, *Philosophical Interrogations* (New York: Harper Torchbooks, 1970), Martin Buber section conducted by Maurice Friedman with Buber's replies trans. by Maurice Friedman, p. 82 f.

Chapter 13 — Is Religion the Enemy of Mankind?

1. Idries Shah, *The way of the Sufi*, "When Death Is Not Death," p. 120; *Tales of the Hasidim: The Later Masters*, "When It Is Good to Deny the Existence of God," p. 89; *Tales of the Hasidim: The Early Masters*, "The Man Who Denies God," p. 134.

2. Martin Buber, *Pointing the Way*, "The Validity and Limitation of the Political Principle," p. 218.